ECONOMICS FOR THE F

Economics for the Rest of Us

DEBUNKING

THE SCIENCE

THAT MAKES LIFE DISMAL

Moshe Adler

THE NEW PRESS

NEW YORK
LONDON

Requests for permission to reproduce selections from this book
should be mailed to: Permissions Department,
The New Press, 38 Greene Street, New York, NY 10013.

Published in the United States by The New Press, New York, 2010
Distributed by Perseus Distribution

LIBRARY OF CONGRESS CATALOGING-IN-PUBLICATION DATA

Adler, Moshe.
Economics for the rest of us : debunking the science that
makes life dismal / Moshe Adler.
p.   cm.
ISBN 978-1-59558-101-3 (hc)
ISBN 978-1-59558-641-4 (pb)
ISBN 978-1-59558-527-1 (e-book)
1. Economics.   2. Income distribution.   3. Wages.   I. Title.
HB71.A235   2009
330—dc22   2009024968

The New Press was established in 1990 as a not-for-profit alternative to the large,
commercial publishing houses currently dominating the book publishing industry.
The New Press operates in the public interest rather than for private gain, and is
committed to publishing, in innovative ways, works of educational, cultural,
and community value that are often deemed insufficiently profitable.

www.thenewpress.com

Composition by dix!

Printed in the United States of America

2   4   6   8   10   9   7   5   3

To the memory of my parents,
Shoshana and Israel

FIGURES

TABLES

INTRODUCTION

Professors of introductory economics are fond of telling their students about the eternal quest for a one-handed economist who would not be able to say, "On the other hand . . ." Is the recession about to end? Economists always waffle on this and similar questions; such predictions can, of course, get them into trouble. But whenever it is necessary to choose sides between the rich and the poor, between the powerful and the powerless, or between workers and corporations, economists are all too often of one mind: according to conventional economic theory, what's good for the rich and the powerful is good for "the economy."

Why is economic theory so one-sided? Is it because anyone who devotes her life to investigating how the economy works inevitably reaches the conclusion that what's good for bosses is good for everybody? Not at all. For every critical economic issue there are competing concepts and theories that lead to different conclusions. The problem is that when they are not missing from textbooks altogether, these theories are almost always summarily dismissed. This would have been of no consequence if the only victims were economics students, but unfortunately most citizens are familiar only with textbook economics, and the economists who influence government policies are, by and large, textbook economists. (Nobel Prize winner Joseph Stiglitz was an exception, but his term as senior vice president and chief economist of the World Bank lasted only three years, from 1997 to 2000).

Economics for the Rest of Us examines the two cornerstones of economics: Part 1 covers economic efficiency and Part 2 covers how wages are determined. The definition of economic efficiency used by economists is covered in the first part of the book because all of economics is centered around it. When economists claim that "the free market is efficient," regardless of how skewed its distribution of resources—or of how much suffering it produces—and when they oppose government intervention to decrease inequality and reduce suffering, it is their definition of efficiency that they rely on. If this were the only valid definition of economic efficiency, economists would perhaps be justified in using it. But, in fact, economists have a choice. An earlier definition of economic efficiency was sensitive to the distribution of income, and this earlier definition suggests that to increase efficiency the government should redistribute resources from the rich to the poor. The definition that economists adopted instead was developed as an attempt to discredit the earlier definition. As we shall see, however, it is not clear that the redistribution version can be discredited so easily.

While economists have managed to convince themselves that the redistribution of income cannot be justified, the rest of the world sees things differently. Practically all governments require the rich to pay higher taxes, and for their part the poor often demand that the government services they get be of the same quality as the services that the rich get, particularly when it comes to education. This forces economists into the sorts of practical debates that their theories were designed to snuff, and in these debates they do not speak with a single voice. As Part 1 shows, some economists argue that the tax rate that the rich pay is inefficiently high because it discourages work, while other economists have conducted empirical research showing that it does not actually have that effect. Similarly, some economists argue that increasing the funding for poor schools would not make a difference because the government will just waste it, while other economists show that this is not the case.

While economists are divided on these important issues, the idea that high taxes are inefficient has nevertheless dominated U.S. tax policy over the last thirty years. As we shall see, what makes this implausible claim appear plausible is the basic model that economists use for analyzing the labor market. The model assumes that employees are free to choose the number of hours that they work, and that when they are paid less they work less. It also assumes that workers do not enjoy work and are shirkers by nature. It is a model of an economy of disconnected individuals who are neither tied to other individuals and to capital in the production process, nor governed by any social norms. In such a model, no outcome can be ruled out and any outcome is equally plausible.

The distribution of income is often thought of as a stage that comes after goods are produced and sold. But it is the distribution of income that determines what and how much will be produced in the first place, and an unequal distribution of income often leads to a decrease in the size of the economic pie. One example is the production and distribution of AIDS drugs. Poor people in developing countries cannot afford these drugs not because they are objectively poor, but because they are *poorer* than people in developed countries. The drug companies choose to price drugs for AIDS beyond the reach of the people of the Third World because it is more profitable to sell these drugs at high prices that only people in the First World can afford, rather than to sell them at low prices all over the world. But as Part I shows, the victims of inequality are not only poor people in the Third World but also middle-income people in the First. Paradoxically, we will see that with the economists' definition of economic efficiency, it is possible to conclude that "the economy" is growing at the same time that most people in that economy have less.

Part II covers theories of wages and of executive compensation, or how inequality is created to begin with. Why does one person make in an hour what another makes in a week or month or year? The "neo-classical" theory that economists have adopted could not be simpler: A person is paid what she is worth to her employer. If she earns $7.25/hour, currently the national minimum wage, then her contribution to her employer is $7.25/hour. And if she is paid many thousands of dollars an hour, then her contribution to her employer is also that much greater.

But this is not the only theory of wages and compensation that exists. The neo-classical theory was invented to replace the "classical" theory, which argued that pay rates are determined not by contributions to production—a meaningless concept, as we will explore—but by the relative bargaining strengths of the different parties. As Part 2 shows, the empirical data supports the classical theory and is inconsistent with the neo-classical theory.

If pay rates are determined by bargaining power, what determines bargaining power? When it comes to workers, laws and government policies play a decisive role. Union rights, the minimum wage law, unemployment insurance, Social Security, welfare, and the enforcement of the rights of immigrants all combine to determine the ability of workers to say no to low wages, and all have been eroded since the 1980s. Part II will make clear the effect of this erosion on workers' well-being.

Unlike workers, executives who bargain with their employers often have the upper hand. And in this case economists have a very good, if simple, explanation for why. The employers of executives are their companies' shareholders, and when each company is owned by a great number of different shareholders, there is nobody to mind the store. As we shall see, this theory is merely an application of the classical theory of wages, which relies on bargaining power to explain rates of pay.

This book is intended for an educated reader with an interest, though not necessarily a background, in economics. It does not use mathematics, though some basic arithmetic does come into play. The aim is to give the reader a thorough understanding of the key concepts and theories of both mainstream economics as well as less-well-known alternatives that often explain economic behavior better than prevailing theories, and that don't always call for policies that benefit the rich and powerful. In each case, the history of economic thought will be traced, along with the historical context that produced the ideas.

Part I

ECONOMIC EFFICIENCY AND THE ROLE OF GOVERNMENT

THE PIE OF HAPPINESS

Economists like to talk about the economy as a pie. A pie is a good way to think about the well-being—or, in the language of early social scientists, happiness—that an economy produces. It turns out that the pie of happiness is largest when the resources of society are distributed equally. Inequality makes the pie smaller.

1.

INCOME EQUALITY:
THE EARLIEST STANDARD OF EFFICIENCY

The search for a definition of economic efficiency began with the emergence of democracy. With democracy came, for the first time in history, the need to ask explicitly whom government should serve. Kings were never bothered by this question. "L'état, c'est moi," Louis XIV of France declared in the early eighteenth century. But who should a government "of the people" and "for the people" serve, when some of the people are rich and some are poor?

In 1793 the French "people" executed Louis XVI and proceeded to ratify in a referendum a constitution that guaranteed income redistribution in the form of public relief and public schooling. ("People" is in quotation marks because not all the French wanted the king executed, nor did all of them vote for the constitution.) But how much should be redistributed? The constitution of 1793 did not say, and the political process that would have determined it was thwarted before it started. A group of citizens, "The Conspiracy of Equals," demanded that the constitution be implemented, but the group was disbanded when its leader, François Noël Babeuf, was sent to the guillotine. The question was addressed theoretically, however, by a contemporary of Babeuf, the wealthy British philosopher Jeremy Bentham (1748–1832).

Bentham based his theory of the efficient degree of redistribution on three building blocks: (i) the happiness of a society consists of the sum of the happiness of each of its members, (ii) an efficient allocation of resources is one that maximizes the happiness of society, and (iii) the happiness that a person gets from an additional dollar (English pound) decreases as the number of dollars that person has increases. In the language of economics, "happiness" has long since been replaced by "utility," and Bentham's theory is known, therefore, as Utilitarianism.

Utility, U, is made of tiny units called "utils." Utils are derived from money. Each additional dollar buys additional utils, and the number of utils that each additional dollar buys is called "the marginal utility of money." The relationship between U and a person's income, I, is shown in figure 1.1. The marginal utility of money is denoted in the figure by ΔU. More income yields more utility, but the relationship is not linear: while an extra dollar always brings additional utility, this additional

FIGURE 1.1: THE UTILITY FUNCTION

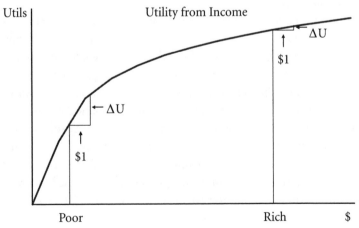

utility gets smaller as a person's income increases. In other words, the marginal utility of money, ΔU, decreases with the amount of money a person has.

A rich person is higher on the utility function than a poor person. Therefore, as figure 1.1 shows, if a dollar is transferred from the rich to the poor, the loss of utility to the rich will be less than the gain in utility to the poor. The transfer of a dollar from the rich person to the poor person will therefore increase the *sum* of utilities of these two individuals. Where should the process of redistribution stop? When each person has the same amount of money, because this will maximize the sum of their utilities. The pie of happiness is biggest—and therefore Utilitarian Efficiency is achieved—when the pie is divided exactly equally.

Definition: Utilitarian-Efficient Policy. A policy is Utilitarian efficient if it maximizes the sum of utilities in society.

Bentham was an effective agitator for equality. At the time, admission to Cambridge and Oxford was limited to students who belonged to the Church of England. When University College London opened in 1826, it was open to all. Bentham was considered the spiritual father of University College and his embalmed body is to this day displayed as a public sculpture there. (The head is now wax because pranksters stole the real head several times.)

But Utilitarianism as a yardstick for economic efficiency did not survive the century in which it was developed. It was supplanted wholly and with complete success by another definition of efficiency, one invented by an Italian economist, Vilfredo Pareto (1848–1923). If Utilitarianism is still mentioned in economics textbooks at all, it is summarily dismissed as a historical curiosity on the way to the truth: Pareto efficiency. How and why did Pareto dismiss Utilitarianism?

FIGURE 1.2: JEREMY BENTHAM, 1748–1832

"The more nearly the actual proportion approaches to equality, the greater will be the mass of happiness."

Credit: Michael Reeve

THE POPE AND PARETO DON'T LIKE IT

Let's begin with the why. At the end of the nineteenth century, inequality in Europe was so extreme that a socialist revolution had become a real possibility. Pope Leo XIII was moved enough by the prevailing economic disparity that in 1891 he issued an encyclical letter, *Rerum Novarum (Of New Things)*, which was devoted to "The Condition of the Working Classes," and in which he wrote:

> The whole process of production as well as trade in every kind of goods has been brought almost entirely under the power of a few, so that a very few rich and exceedingly rich men have laid a yoke almost of slavery on the unnumbered masses of non-owning workers.[1]

This would seem to lay the groundwork for a call to redistribute "the whole process of production." In fact, though, the pope objected strongly to redistribution through the power of the state. The rich should have no legal obligation to assist the poor, the pope claimed: "These [assisting the poor] are duties not of justice, except in cases of extreme need, but of Christian charity, which obviously cannot be enforced by legal action." In a book published in 1906, *Manual of Political Economy*, Pareto elaborated on why assistance to the poor cannot be legally mandated, warning against even a mild redistribution by the state because of the slippery slope:

> Those who demanded equality of taxes to aid the poor did not imagine that there would be a progressive tax at the expense of the rich, and a system in which the taxes are voted by those who do not pay them, so that one sometimes hears the following reasoning shamelessly made: "Tax A falls only on wealthy persons and it will be used for expenditures which will be useful only to the less fortunate; thus it will surely be approved by the majority of voters."[2]

But why was Pareto opposed to redistribution? Because according to him Bentham was not necessarily right. As figure 1.1 shows, Bentham assumed that the only difference between a rich person and poor person was in how much money they had: given the same amounts of money they would have exactly the same amounts of utility. It is this similarity between the rich and the poor that led Bentham to conclude that transferring a dollar from the rich to the poor would hurt the rich less than it would help the poor. But according to Pareto rich people and poor people may be fundamentally different. In this scenario transferring money from the rich to the poor could actually hurt the rich more than it would help the poor. He used an extreme hypothetical example to illustrate this possibility. What if the rich actually enjoy the poverty of the poor? He asked. Then reducing poverty by redistribution may hurt the rich more than it would help the poor, Pareto argued. "Assume a collectivity made up of a wolf and a sheep," Pareto explained. "The happiness of the wolf consists in eating the sheep, that of the sheep in not being eaten. How is this collectivity to be made happy?"[3]

Economists do not usually cite this passage in explaining Pareto's objection to Utilitarianism. Instead they ask what if the rich and the poor do not have the same utility function, as in figure 1.1, but instead, by chance, the rich happen to derive *greater* utility from a given quantity of money than the poor do. Figure 1.3 depicts this argument graphically, and it shows that a transfer of a dollar from the rich to the poor in this case may hurt the rich more than it would help the poor. Notice that just like a poor person, a rich person also derives greater utility from her first dollar than from her last one. But a rich person's utility from her last dollar may exceed the poor person's utility from her first dollar.

What would happen if all of a sudden the rich and the poor traded places, and the rich became poor and the poor became rich? In this case the curves in figure 1.3 would stay the same, but their labels would

FIGURE 1.3: UTILITY FUNCTIONS OF THE RICH AND THE POOR

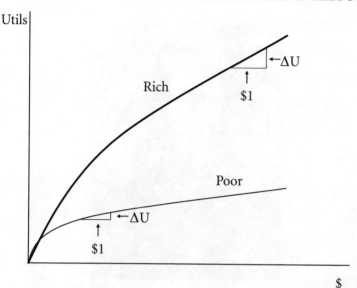

change: the lower curve would become the utility function of the rich and the upper curve would become the utility function of the poor. In this case, transferring money from the rich to the poor would increase the sum of utilities and redistribution would be justified.

Economists do not claim that the situation as it is described in figure 1.3 actually exists in reality, only that it may exist. Because utility is not measurable, this possibility simply cannot be ruled out. And if this is indeed the situation, then Bentham's argument does not hold, and redistribution is therefore not justified. Bentham acknowledged this possibility. "Difference of character is inscrutable," he said.[4] But, he argued, a large difference in character between the rich and the poor was so unlikely that the government would make fewer mistakes if it operated

FIGURE 1.4: VILFREDO PARETO, 1848–1923

"Assume a collectivity made up of a wolf and a sheep. . . . How is this collectivity to be made happy?"

under the assumption that the rich and the poor are similar, than if it operated under the assumption that they are fantastically different. The economist Abba Lerner (1903–82) noted that Bentham was just applying the first principle of statistics: when it is not known that things that appear the same are really different, the best we can do is to assume that they are the same.[5] This is why we assign the probability of $\frac{1}{6}$ to each face of a die.

Unlike Bentham or Lerner, Pareto did not concern himself with the question of how *likely* it was that redistribution would hurt the rich more than it would help the poor. For him this theoretical possibility, no matter how remote, was reason enough to reject the lever of equality as a yardstick of economic efficiency. And based solely on this theoretical possibility, the entire economics profession removed the distribution of resources from its definition of economic efficiency and replaced it with Pareto's own definition.

2

EQUALITY DOES NOT MATTER:
PARETO EFFICIENCY AND THE FREE MARKET

Like Bentham, Pareto also equated efficiency with maximizing the well-being produced by society's resources. But while Bentham allowed for the possibility that this would require the redistribution of these resources from the rich to the poor, Pareto ruled this possibility out from the start. According to him, an allocation of resources is (Pareto) efficient if it cannot be changed in a way that will make at least one person better off without making anybody else worse off. This definition is indifferent to the distribution of society's resources.

But first it is necessary to explain what the definition actually means. The next few pages are the most technical in the book, and it is my hope that readers will bear with them. The concept of Pareto efficiency is a critical building block of all modern-day economics, and a few extra minutes spent mastering this slightly arcane material will be well rewarded. The graphs are helpful, but not essential, to understanding the ideas under discussion. The rest of the book will be far less technical by comparison.

SUPPLY AND DEMAND

The economist's analysis of the behavior of the free market begins with, on the one hand, the quantity of a commodity that is available for consumption, and on the other, the different values that different consumers place on this commodity. In other words, it begins with supply and demand.[1]

Suppose that seven families, A to G, need housing in a city, and suppose also that there are only six apartments available for rent. All the apartments are identical in terms of desirability, and each apartment is owned by a different landlord. Each family has a different level of income, and therefore the maximum amount that it is willing to pay for an apartment is also different. The maximum amount that a family is willing to pay for an apartment is called the family's *reservation price*. The reservation prices are shown in table 2.1, and as we shall see, they form the demand for a commodity.

Two factors determine a family's reservation price for a given apartment: the family's income, and the best available alternative, in terms of quality, location, and rent. For instance, in our example, if family G does not get one of the six apartments in the city, it will have to live in an apartment outside the city for which it will have to pay $1,200/month. It is in view of this alternative that family G's reservation price for the city apartment is $1,500/month. This means that if the rent for a city apartment is actually $1,500/month, family G is indifferent between living in the city apartment and living in the alternative apartment for $1,200/month.

TABLE 2.1: RESERVATION RENTS

FAMILY	A	B	C	D	E	F	G
Reservation Price	$6,000	$5,250	$4,500	$3,750	$3,000	$2,250	$1,500

Who will get the six apartments and how much will the rent for the apartments be? If each apartment is owned by a different landlord and neither landlords nor tenants collude, and, in addition, if what each family pays for its apartment is public information, then the market is a "competitive market."[2] The first thing to notice about the competitive market is that it forces the rent on all the apartments to be the same. To see why, suppose that the rents are not the same. For instance, suppose that family A pays $2,000/month while family B pays only $1,500/month, and that these rents are common knowledge. In this case the landlord of family B would try to entice family A to her apartment with a rent offer that is lower than family A's rent but higher than family B's rent. A rent of $1,750/month would be agreeable to both parties. Alternatively, it could be family A who would initiate the transaction by offering to pay more than family B for the apartment that family B is occupying. Again, $1,750 would make both parties (family A and the landlord) better off. Such competition between landlords (who "steal" tenants from one another) and between tenants (who "steal" apartments from one another) will continue until the rent on the two apartments is identical. No tenant would want to pay more than other tenants do and no landlord would want to receive less than other landlords do, and as a result we get the Law of One Price:

In a competitive market identical goods have an identical price.

What would this unique rent be?

The minimum rent has to be at least $1500.01/month, because if it were lower, say $1,499/month, then seven families would have wanted apartments even though there are only six available. In this case the "homeless" family would have offered one of the landlords more than $1,499/month for an apartment (say $1,499.50), that landlord would have accepted the offer, and the existing tenant would have been evicted. The competition between consumers for apartments will not stop until the price rises sufficiently to force the poorest family out of the competition altogether. That means that the rent must be at least $1,500.01.

The same logic also makes it clear that the market rent cannot be higher than $2,250/month, because if it were, one of the landlords would be without a tenant, and she would then compete for a tenant by lowering her rent. Competition between landlords will stop only when each has a tenant, and that means that the rent must be at a level that is below the reservation price of family F. Hence, the market rent will be between $1,500.01 and $2,250.

The reservation prices can be used to draw the "demand curve," which shows how many apartments are demanded at each price (figure 2.1). For instance, the curve shows that when the rent is between $2,250.01 and $3,000/month, five apartments are demanded. (The demand curve is continuous, as if it is possible to have a fraction of an apartment. This is done merely for convenience and does not change the analysis at all.) The supply curve in our case is even simpler, because it is just a vertical line that represents the six apartments that landlords want to rent out. The intersection between the supply and the demand curves gives the "equilibrium" prices, the range of the prices that "clear" the market.

Definition: Market-Clearing Price: A price "clears" the market, or is an "equilibrium price," if all the apartments that are supplied at that price have tenants and all the tenants that are willing to pay that price have apartments.

Family G does not have an apartment, but the market is in equilibrium nevertheless because at the equilibrium price the family "does not want" (cannot afford) an apartment.

FIGURE 2.1: THE SUPPLY AND DEMAND OF APARTMENTS

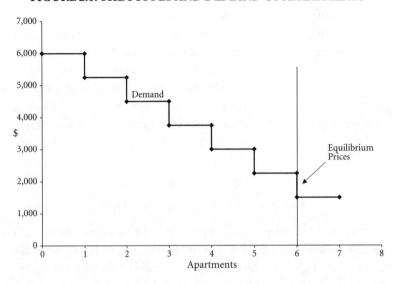

CONSUMER SURPLUS AND PARETO EFFICIENCY

A family rents an apartment only when its reservation price for the apartment is higher than the market price (when the market is in equilibrium, the market price is also the equilibrium price). The difference between what the apartment is worth to the family and the rent the family has to pay is a measure of the net benefit to the family from its apartment. This benefit is called the "consumer surplus." For example, when the market rent is $1,750/month, family C earns a consumer surplus of $2,750 from the apartment because its reservation price is $4,500. (Assume that the price of a slice of pizza is $2.50. If your reservation price for a slice is $3.00 then your consumer surplus is fifty cents. If your reservation price is exactly $2.50 then you are indifferent between buying and not buying it;

regardless of what you do, your consumer surplus then is zero. Finally, if your reservation price is less than $2.50, you do not buy the slice. In other words, you buy a slice only when this will make you either strictly better off or not worse off than not buying it.) We shall see that the allocation of apartments to families that the free market produces *maximizes the sum of consumer surpluses in the economy,* which is why this allocation is Pareto efficient. By contrast, the allocation of apartments to families that rent control produces may result in a smaller sum of consumer surpluses, and this is why rent control is Pareto inefficient. Instead of utils, Pareto measures efficiency in terms of "consumer surplus."

RENT CONTROL: A CASE STUDY

Rent control is a form of government intervention designed to assist middle-class and poor families that would otherwise be priced out by the free market. This is, for instance, the situation in New York City today, where a form of rent control is in effect, and where there is little doubt that without this control, thousands of families would not be able to afford their homes. Yet for modern economists rent control is the quintessential example of a policy that is not Pareto efficient. In fact, the first chapter of one of the most popular contemporary economics textbooks, *Intermediate Microeconomics* by Hal Varian, uses rent control to illustrate Pareto inefficiency. Rent control is not Pareto efficient, we shall see, because it lets middle-class families live in apartments they otherwise could not afford, and because it therefore does not maximize the sum of consumer surpluses.

Let's continue our example of the housing market by supposing that the government adopts a rent-control policy that imposes a rent cap of $500/month on all apartments, and let's suppose that as a result, family G has an apartment and family A does not. Is this situation Pareto efficient? The answer depends on whether it is *potentially* possible to reallocate an apartment from family G to family A and make at least one of the families better off without making the other family worse off. The answer is that *potentially* it is possible.

To see how, suppose that subletting rent-controlled apartments for any price is legal. Family A could offer family G a sum that is more than $1,500/month for the apartment, which would fully compensate family G for giving up its apartment (and moving to the suburbs) and still be less than family A's own reservation price of $6,000/month. Both families would thus be better off. For instance, say that the sublet rent is $4,000/month. Then family G's consumer surplus from the apartment (in which it no longer lives) is $3,500/month (because the landlord gets $500/month) and family A's consumer surplus from the apartment (in which it now lives) is $2,000/month. Both families would be better off, without any family or landlord being worse off. We conclude, therefore, that if under rent control a poor family ends up with an apartment that a rich family wants, rent control is Pareto inefficient.[3]

On the other hand, if all the apartments went to the wealthiest families to begin with—as they would if the market were free—the allocation of apartments *would* be Pareto efficient. The reason is that, in this scenario, even if subletting were legal, the allocation of apartments would not change. The poor do not have the money that the rich would demand to vacate their apartments. Of course, it is precisely because the free market allocates apartments in a way that is Pareto efficient that rent control exists to begin with.[4]

Figure 2.2 depicts Pareto efficiency diagrammatically. Since the reservation price of family A for an apartment is $6,000/month and the rent that the landlord collects is $500/month, the maximum consumer surplus that a rent-controlled apartment can generate is $5,500; the figure shows how this surplus can be divided between families A and G. If family A gets the apartment to begin with, then the allocation is point *a* in the figure: the consumer surplus of family A is $5,500/month, while the consumer surplus of family G is $0. If family G gets the apartment to begin with and continues living in it, then the allocation is point *g*: the consumer surplus of family G is $1,000, and the consumer surplus of family A is $0. If family G gets the apartment to begin with and then sublets it, then the apartment generates a surplus of $5,500/month for the two families together. In that case the families are somewhere on the line labeled "Pareto Frontier."

The "Pareto Frontier" gets its name from the fact that at any point on

FIGURE 2.2: DIVIDING THE PIE

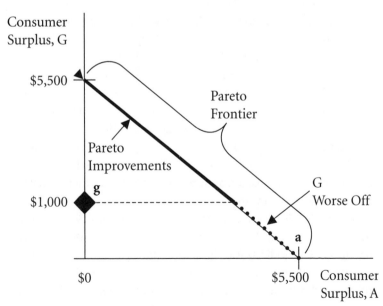

it the sum of the surpluses of families A and G is at its maximum possible level ($5,500), and it is not possible, therefore, to increase the surplus of one family without reducing the surplus of the other. Point g is not on the frontier because if the families start at that point (Family G gets the apartment), then it is possible to make both families better off at the same time by moving away from it. Of course, since family G gets a consumer surplus of $1,000 from the apartment, it would not agree to give it up unless it is paid at least $1,000 above the rent of $500. In the diagram, Family G would only agree to be on the section of the Pareto Frontier labeled "Pareto Improvements." (A reallocation of resources is a "Pareto improvement" if it makes at least one person better off without making anybody worse off. In a Pareto improvement there are no losers and at least one winner.) The fact that point g is not on the Pareto frontier is why economists conclude that rent control is not Pareto efficient.

Figure 2.3 shows the effect of rent control when the consumer surpluses that families A and G derive from all goods and services are considered. With rent control, the families are at point g, inside the Pareto frontier. Potentially, if rent control is abolished the families could be anywhere on the Pareto frontier. But in fact they will be at point a. In dollars, G's loss will be small ($1,000), but because of its poverty, G will lose about one-third of its total consumer surplus. In dollars, A's gain will be large ($5,500), but as percent of its total consumer surplus the gain will be small.

KALDOR, HICKS, AND COST-BENEFIT ANALYSIS

When poor families occupy rent-controlled apartments that the rich want, legalizing subletting would increase the well-being of both poor and rich. Why isn't subletting legal then? Because the purpose of rent control is to maintain neighborhoods that are economically mixed.

FIGURE 2.3: RENT CONTROL, THE BIG PICTURE

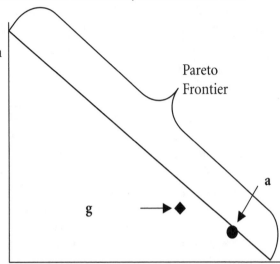

Gs Consume r
Surpluses from
All Goods and
Services

Pareto
Frontier

a

g

A's Consumer
Surpluses from
All Goods and
Services

When poor families get housing under rent-control rules that do not allow subletting, the allocation of apartments is not Pareto efficient. But should rent control be abolished even if the families who occupy rent-controlled apartments would be offered no compensation (a move from *g* to *a* in Figure 2.2)? Because abolishing rent control would make one of the families worse off, the concept of Pareto efficiency does not provide us with any guidelines about what to do. Pareto's definition tells us that the government should adopt policies that make everybody better off, but regarding policies that produce losers in addition to winners, the definition is silent. The problem is, however, that in reality most, if not all, government policies produce losers in addition to winners. As a guide to policy, therefore, Pareto efficiency is useless.

In this respect Utilitarianism is, of course, very different. Utilitarianism calls for redistributive policies, which, by their very nature, produce losers. Economists reject Utilitarianism because it compares the utility levels of the rich and the poor (and argues that a transfer of a dollar from the rich to the poor would help the latter more than it would hurt the former). Comparing the utilities of different individuals is not permissible, these modern economists argue. But without comparing the utilities of the winners with the utilities of the losers, how can policies be analyzed? As the economist Roy Harrod (1900–1978) explained in 1938: "if the incomparability of utility to different individuals is strictly pressed [i.e., if utilities are incomparable], not only are the prescriptions of the welfare school [Utilitarianism] ruled out, but all prescriptions whatever. The economist as an adviser is completely stultified, and unless his speculations be regarded as of paramount aesthetic value, he had better be suppressed completely." [5]

The English economists Nicholas Kaldor (1908–86) and John Hicks (1904–89) volunteered, therefore, to infuse policy content into Pareto's definition of efficiency. According to Kaldor a policy should be implemented whenever the cumulative gains from it would exceed the cumulative losses, *regardless of whether the losers would be compensated for their losses.* Otherwise the policy should not be implemented:

> There is no need for the economist to prove—as indeed he never could prove—that as a result of the adoption of a certain measure nobody in the community is going to suffer. In order to establish his case [that the measure should be adopted], it is quite sufficient for him to show that even if all those who suffer as a result are fully compensated for their loss [by the

winners], the rest of the community will still be better off than before. Whether the [losers] should in fact be given compensation or not, is a political question on which the economist, qua economist, could hardly pronounce an opinion.[6]

Hicks's test is similar in its approach but different in its specifics.[7] According to Hicks, a policy should *not* be implemented whenever the losers from the implementation could compensate the winners for forgoing the implementation and still be at least as well off themselves, regardless of whether the compensation would actually take place. Otherwise the policy should be implemented.

In order to see what the Kaldor and the Hicks tests actually mean, we continue with our housing example. Assume that all six available apartments are rent-controlled and are occupied by the poorest families, B–G; each family pays the controlled rent of $500/month. Assume also that without rent control the rents would be $2,000/month. (We saw earlier that the market rent must lie between $1,500.01/month and $2,250/month.) If rent control were abolished, family G would lose its apartment altogether; in terms of consumer surplus its loss would be $1,000/month (the difference between its $1,500 reservation price and the $500 rent it was paying under rent control). Families B–F would continue to live in their apartments, but each family would lose $1,500/month because of the higher rent.

Let's apply Kaldor's test first. The test asks the following question: If rent control were abolished and all the losers were compensated for their losses, would the rest of the community be better off? In order to compensate families B–F for the higher rent, the rent increase could simply be rebated back to them by their landlords. This would leave these families and their landlords just as well-off as they were before the abolition of rent control, but the rest of the community—families A and G and the landlord of family G—would all be better off. The landlord would be better off because she would collect $1,500/month in extra rent. Family A would be better off because after paying a rent of $2,000/month to the landlord and a compensation of $2,000/month to family G it would still enjoy a consumer surplus of $2,000/month. And family G would be better off because its consumer surplus from the apartment would be $2,000/month instead of $1,000/month. With some winners and no losers, rent control *should* be abolished, according to Kaldor's test.

Let's turn now to the Hicks test, which asks the following question: Would the losers from the abolition of rent control be better off compensating the winners for agreeing to forgo it, or would they be better off resigning themselves to its abolition? Two parties stand to win from the abolition of rent control: The landlords and family A. The parties that stand to lose are families B–G. Of these, families B–F could in fact compensate the landlords for forgoing the abolition of rent control. They could agree to pay the market rent of $2,000/month even when rent control continues, and both they and the landlords would be just as well off as if rent control were abolished. But they would not agree to pay anything toward compensating family A, because if they had to pay more they would be better off without rent control. Family G would not be able to compensate even its landlord, because its surplus from the apartment is only $1,000/month, less than the required $1,500/month increase in rent. Thus, as a group, the losers from the abolition of rent control could not compensate the winners for forgoing it, and rent control should therefore be abolished according to the Hicks test as well.

Kaldor's and Hicks's tests lead to the same allocation of resources that the free market would produce. This is no accident. These are really no more than tests of whether or not policies lead to the free market allocation of resources. Their only "advantage" over the actual definition of Pareto efficiency is that while Pareto efficiency calls for abolishing a redistributive policy only when the poor would be compensated for their losses, Kaldor and Hicks call for the abolition of redistributive policies regardless of what happens to the poor.

Economists call the calculations of whether a policy passes the Kaldor-Hicks tests cost-benefit analysis. For example, in the analysis of whether rent control should be abolished, the "benefits" are the consumer surpluses that the rich would gain and the "costs" are the consumer surpluses that the poor would lose. In 1981 President Reagan signed an executive order that required all federal agencies to conduct cost-benefit analysis of all their regulations. President Clinton renewed the requirement with another executive order in 1994. "Circular A-4" of the Office of Management and Budget explains the need for cost-benefit analysis in the following way:

> Benefit-cost analysis is a primary tool used for regulatory analysis. Where all benefits and costs can be quantified and expressed in monetary units, benefit-cost analysis provides decision makers with a clear indication of the most efficient alternative. . . . [This] is the alternative that generates the largest net benefits to society (ignoring distributional effects). This is useful information for decision makers and the public to receive, even when economic efficiency is not the only or the overriding public policy objective.[8]

One problem with this logical-sounding statement is that the benefits and the costs, which are measured in consumer surpluses, are themselves determined by the distribution of income. The benefits from abolishing rent control would exceed the costs for no other reason than that the rich can pay more for apartments than the poor. Thus, unlike Utilitarianism, which "arbitrarily" reaches the conclusion that the rich and the poor deserve the same of everything, cost-benefit analysis "objectively" determines that the rich deserve more.[9]

PARETO EFFICIENCY IN PRODUCTION

To economists, rent control is also the perfect example of how price controls impede the emergence of Pareto efficiency with respect to the production of goods. Rent control reduces the profits of landlords, the argument goes, and therefore it reduces the landlords' incentive to acquire new housing units. The ensuing reduction in the level of construction constitutes a Pareto inefficiency because consumers and landlords would benefit from more housing. Of course, some tenants would lose their apartments if rent control were abolished, but the gains to the landlords and tenants from the new housing would probably far outweigh the loss in consumer surpluses of the displaced tenants; if so, the losers could *potentially* be compensated for their losses.

The first problem with this argument is that it does not account for why a government might impose price controls in a particular market to begin with. In the Middle Ages the price of bread was controlled everywhere in Europe, but today the price of bread is not controlled anywhere.[10] Why? The answer is that in medieval times there wasn't enough food to satisfy the demands of both rich and poor people, but today there is. Of course, the controls did not make more bread available, but they did make more bread available to the poor. (They also forced everybody to stand in line. When the price of a good is so low that the poor can afford it, but the quantity supplied is less than the quantity demanded, a line is formed.) Thus price controls are imposed on a free market when poor consumers believe that the free market allocates to them less than their fair share of a good, and when they are able to demand that the situation be rectified. (In the Middle Ages the poor did not have a venue for demanding anything, but the authorities were wary of riots.)

The second problem with the Pareto inefficiency in production argument is that it does not say what to do during the transition period that the free market needs to produce the promised abundance. Abolishing rent control will result in the displacement of many families for the promise that at some time in the future they and additional families will be better off. Even if this promise is to be kept, the economist John Maynard Keynes (1883–1946) warned against simply waiting for the free market to solve economic problems because, "in the long run we are all dead." What should be done with the families that would be uprooted if rent controls were abolished?

The third problem with the Pareto inefficiency in production argument is that the incentives to build new housing and to maintain the old can easily be established while keeping the price controls in place. New construction is usually exempted from rent control, and landlords of rent-controlled apartments are permitted to raise the rents to cover any increases in the cost of maintenance.

An example of how economists use Pareto efficiency in production to argue against redistributive policies comes from a *Primetime Live* segment about rent regulation in New York City that ABC Television ran in 1997, when rent control came under serious attack. The program featured as an expert the economist Walter Williams, chair of the economics department at George Mason University at the time. Williams lived in Virginia, not New York, and had done no research about the housing market in the city. In his analysis he presented no numbers about rent control in New York or in any other place in the world. Instead of giving viewers the facts about rent control, host John Stossel broadcast footage of different rent-regulated buildings in NYC and Williams commented on what he saw. Stossel started by showing Williams photographs of rich and famous people who live in posh rent-stabilized apartments. He then showed his guest pictures of dilapidated buildings in the Bronx.

> Stossel: Finally, the most destructive unintended consequence of rent control is that some landlords say, "If I can't raise the rent, I won't make repairs." And they don't.
> Williams: Short of aerial bombardment the best way to destroy a city is rent control.[11]

Landlords "won't make repairs"? Wasn't Williams just told of posh rent-stabilized apartments of the rich and famous, and shouldn't Stossel have concluded that what determined the condition of the buildings was not rent control but the wealth of the tenants? Anyone with any knowledge about the real estate market in New York City knows that the reason landlords cannot raise the rents in poor neighborhoods is not rent control but . . . that the tenants are poor. While hard statistics are not available,[12] anecdotal evidence indicates that in poor neighborhoods in New York City the market rents are frequently *below* the regulated rents. The problem of low-quality housing for the poor in New York City is not new. If Stossel wanted to show viewers what an unregulated free market in housing can do the quality of housing in New York City, he could have used the photographs in Jacob Riis's 1890 book *How the Other Half Lives*. It is precisely the failure of the free market to provide acceptable quality housing to the poor that led to the creation of housing codes.

Rent control is akin to "aerial bombardment"? In the booming New York City of 1997? Williams should have told viewers that all new construction in New York City is exempt from rent regulations and that in spite of rent regulations, new housing is being built everywhere in the city. What is being destroyed, however, is low-income housing, and not by rent control, but by income inequality. The prices of luxury apartments in Manhattan are so high that developers have no incentive to build new low-income housing. In fact, as will be shown below, existing low-income housing is often converted into luxury housing. Concerning maintenance, Williams might have informed viewers that New York's regulated rents are adjusted annually to compensate landlords for increases in maintenance costs. Finally, Williams might have also told the viewers that landlords who bought their buildings after rent regulations went into effect paid prices that reflected the existence of rent regulations. Their rate of return on their investment is therefore the same as on free market properties.

It would be tempting to dismiss Williams as a lone economist. But a survey of economists who are members of the American Economic Association showed that 76 percent generally agree with the statement that "a ceiling on rents reduces the quality and quantity of housing available," and an additional 17 percent agree with this statement "with provisos." [13] This is not exactly the same as declaring an opposition to rent control, but that's exactly how this result is being widely interpreted, and the interpretation is probably correct. Even Williams's outlandish comparison of rent control to aerial bombardment is not original; economists often parrot it regarding rent control, although unlike Williams, they usually attribute it to its author, the Swedish economist Assar Lindbeck (b. 1930). [14] (An example of the damage that the study of economics can inflict, since Lindbeck is a socialist.)

RENT CONTROL FOR THE RICH?

The argument that rent control is Pareto inefficient is not the argument that gets media attention. What does generate a buzz is the claim that rent-regulated apartments go to rich tenants. The actress Mia Farrow became the poster girl for all that is wrong with rent control because she, a

famous and rich actress, occupied a rent-regulated apartment overlooking Central Park, and Stossel, of course, did not fail to mention her. So do
rent-regulated apartments go to the rich?

Stossel's anecdotes notwithstanding, the evidence shows that, as a
rule, they don't. New York renters are poor in general, but tenants in
rent-regulated apartments are even poorer. The median income of a
renter household in a rent-stabilized apartment in 2004 was $32,000.
The median income of a renter household in a market-rent apartment,
on the other hand, was $42,000, almost a third higher.[15]

The use of Mia Farrow as a poster girl *against* rent control is interesting, because she could have been the poster girl for the other side. In 1994
the rent-regulation law in New York was changed, and all apartments
that rent for more than $2,000/month became deregulated if the income
of their tenants exceeded $250,000 a year. (In 1997 the law was changed
again: an apartment became decontrolled—i.e., went to market-level
rent—if its rent was higher than $2,000 and the income of the tenant ex-
ceeded $175,000, and any apartment that became vacant with a rent of
more than $2,000 became automatically decontrolled, regardless of the
income of the new tenant.) Did Farrow simply pay the market rent so
that she could stay in her apartment? She left the city altogether. Why?
Most probably because she could not afford to stay. Farrow has fourteen
kids, several of whom were adopted with severe disabilities (blindness,
heart ailment, cerebral palsy, paralysis). It is not surprising, then, that
even she could not afford Manhattan's market rents.

The Farrows left, and another family occupies their apartment now.
Does the family that replaced the Farrows also have fourteen kids, and do
these kids have as many special needs as the Farrow kids do? No newspaper ran a story on the family that replaced the Farrows. Since the new
family pays the market rent for the apartment, this must be proof that it
is more deserving of it than the Farrows. When a policy benefits the poor,

everybody is a utilitarian, calculating whether the beneficiaries are deserving. No calculations are carried out, however, when the rich gobble up the resources of society.

Mia Farrow's case notwithstanding, it may still be argued that the eligibility for rent-controlled apartments should be limited to low-income families. Because government programs that benefit only the poor often perish, this argument is not as clear-cut as it may at first appear. But the danger of basing policy on anecdotes instead of hard data is clear.

REDISTRIBUTION, PARETO, AND PARETO EFFICIENCY

The redistribution of goods is not Pareto efficient because it gives goods to people who have low reservation prices for them. But every person, rich or poor, has the same reservation price for money: a dollar is worth exactly a dollar to both rich and poor. Thus the redistribution of money cannot be objected to on Pareto efficiency grounds. Pareto objected to the redistribution of money not because it violated his definition of efficiency, but because of the possibility that total utility in society will decrease if a dollar is passed from the rich to the poor.

3

THE PARETO EFFICIENCY COPS

Economists often fill official posts, and when they do, they dutifully apply what they have learned: if it is not Pareto efficient, abolish it.

IT IS NOT PARETO EFFICIENT: THE POOR EAT TOO MUCH

In 1997 several Asian countries experienced a financial crisis that started when foreign investors slowed the pace of their investments in these countries. Currency speculators understood that with fewer dollars coming in, the value of the local currencies would fall, and they converted their holdings of local currencies into dollars. This caused local residents to fear for the value of their own savings, and they too started converting their local currencies into the dollars that were fast disappearing. The end result of this self-fulfilling prophecy was an increase in the value of the dollar.

There is no good explanation for why foreign investors all of a sudden lost their confidence in the abilities of the Asian economies to continue to grow. John Maynard Keynes, the English economist of the Great Depression, argued that the moods of investors defy explanation. He attributed these mood swings to an "animalistic spirit" that is unpredictable. But regardless of whether there is a rational explanation, the fact remains that the value of the dollar increased, which meant an immediate increase in the local-currency price of imports.

Indonesia was particularly hard hit by the crisis because it relies heavily on food imports: all of Indonesia's wheat, one-third of its sugar, and one-tenth of its rice are imported.[1] The government of Indonesia subsidized food prices at the time, but despite these subsidies food prices increased so much that food riots engulfed the country; five hundred people died in the capital, Jakarta, alone. To feed its people Indonesia needed a loan from the International Monetary Fund (IMF).

The fact that the Indonesian government traditionally subsidized the price of food did not sit well with the IMF economists. As will be explained below, food subsidies violate Pareto efficiency. So, amid the riots and with the backing of Larry Summers, the deputy U.S. secretary of the treasury at the time, the IMF demanded that Indonesia abolish its food subsidies to establish "market-based pricing" as a condition of receiving the loan. President Clinton even called President Suharto of Indonesia from Air Force One to demand that he comply with the IMF's demands. And comply he did.[2]

Food subsidies may not be Pareto efficient for the same reason that rent control is not Pareto efficient: poor people are being given access to goods they otherwise could not afford. Table 3.1 below shows a poor family's reservation prices for food when it has an income of $20. The first two units of food are biological necessity. If the price of food is $20/unit, the family will buy one unit, and if the price of food is $10/unit it will buy two units. We assume that the world market price of food is $20/unit, and that this is the price that the Indonesian government pays. The government sells the food to its citizens at $5/unit, providing a subsidy of $15/unit. After the first two, biologically necessary units, the third unit is optional, and the family does have a reservation price for that and all additional units, given that particular subsidy.

TABLE 3.1: A FAMILY'S NECESSITY AND RESERVATION PRICES FOR FOOD

Unit	1	2	3	4
Reservation Price	Any Price	Any Price	$6	$4

From the table it is clear that without the price subsidy the poor family would buy one unit of food for $20 and go hungry. With the subsidy it would buy three units. The family's consumer surplus from the third unit is $1.00 yet the government spends $15.00 to generate it. This means that the subsidy produces an allocation of resources that is Pareto inefficient. Theoretically the government could abolish the subsidy for the third unit and give the poor family $2.00 in cash instead; the poor family would then consume only two units of food and be $1.00 better off this way, while the taxpayer will be $13.00 better off, a Pareto improvement.

In practice it is impossible to cancel the subsidies on only one of the units that a family buys. If the subsidy is cancelled on all the units and the family is given a cash transfer of $42, the situation will be the same as above: the family will be $1 better off with the transfer than with the subsidy, and the taxpayers will be $13 better off (since the subsidy on three units is $45).

While in our example the food subsidy is Pareto inefficient, this result holds only for a family that is sufficiently affluent. Consider a family with an income of only $10. With the food subsidy the family buys two units. No Pareto improvement is possible in this case because cutting food consumption will result in malnourishment; the subsidy is therefore Pareto efficient.

Food subsidies enjoy strong support in poor countries because they benefit a large number of people (the rich do not benefit from them because they pay for the subsidies through their taxes). Normally, however, if the subsidies were abolished, only the poorest among the beneficiaries would be eligible for compensation. And since the poorest citizens are politically weak, compensation for all who need it rarely materializes. The result of abolishing food subsidies is therefore often hunger. It is not surprising, then, that the abolition of the subsidies in Indonesia led to riots.

The Nobel Prize–winning economist Joseph Stiglitz, who was the chief economist of the World Bank at the time, called the food riots in Indonesia "the IMF Riots." "When a nation is down and out," Stiglitz told the *Observer*, "the IMF takes advantage and squeezes the last pound of blood out of them. They turn up the heat until finally the whole cauldron blows up." The *Observer* obtained secret IMF documents in which the Fund's managers revealed that they actually *expected* "social unrest" in response to the policies they would impose, and that they decided to respond to these riots with "political resolve."[3]

The Utilitarian View

How does utilitarianism apply to food subsidies? If the losers from the abolition of the subsidies will be fully compensated for their losses, the subsidies should be abolished. The question is whether the subsidies should be abolished without compensation. If without the subsidies poor people will experience hunger, it is clear that the gain in utility from the subsidies to the poor would exceed the loss in utility to the rich who would pay for them. Of course, utils are not measurable. Weighting the relative gains and losses requires judgment, and mistakes are possible. But food subsidies may be Utilitarian efficient even if they are not Pareto efficient.

FIGURE 3.1: LARRY SUMMERS, 1954–

"The economic logic behind dumping a load of toxic waste in the lowest wage country is impeccable."

Credit: Stephanie Mitchell/Harvard Photographic Services/Redux

IT IS NOT PARETO EFFICIENT:
THE POOR VISIT THE DOCTOR TOO MANY TIMES

In 2004 the economist Martin Feldstein, who had served as President
Reagan's chair of the Council of Economic Advisers, received the highest
recognition that economists give to one of their own: presidency of the
American Economic Association. Feldstein devoted a large part of his
presidential address to health insurance. Health insurance is, of course, a
very fitting topic for the president of the American Economic Association to address, since some fifty million Americans are without health insurance despite the fact that many of them work full-time.[4] Given the
crisis in health care, one might have expected Feldstein to talk about how
to provide health insurance to more Americans or, perhaps, how to remove the unhealthy limitations on health care put in place by HMOs.
But what Feldstein told the audience instead was that health insurance in
United States faces a problem because deductibles and co-payments are
too low, and as a result people go to the doctor too many times: "They
[low co-payments] also lead to an increased demand for care that is
worth less than its cost of production."[5]

To a noneconomist, the prime example of inefficient medical care
would probably be cosmetic surgery, because it diverts doctors, nurses,
and operating rooms away from real medical problems. But to an economist, cosmetic surgery is actually the prime example of *efficient* medical
care. Why? Precisely because it is not medically necessary. Because it is
not necessary, it is not covered by insurance, and without insurance a
patient will never have cosmetic surgery unless he is able to pay for it.
This guarantees that the surgery is not "worth less than its cost of production." Real medical care is covered by insurance, and this is why,
according to Martin Feldstein, it may be "worth less than its cost of
production."

The following example illustrates Feldstein's argument that low co-payments lead to medical care that is "worth less than its cost of production." Suppose that the cost of a doctor's visit is $100 and that Poor, who is uninsured, cannot pay more than $20 for the visit. This means that Poor's reservation price for the visit is $20 and the doctor's visit will not take place. Let's change the example a bit, however, by assuming that Poor is insured, and that there is no co-payment. Under these circumstances the visit would take place, even though it is "worth less than its cost of production." Is the visit Pareto inefficient? In other words, had the insurance company offered Poor a sum that is less than the cost of the visit—say, $95—*not* to visit the doctor, would Poor have accepted it? It would be wrong to simply assume that she would, because while Poor could not afford to pay more than $20 for the visit had she had to pay for it herself, she may nevertheless prefer to see the doctor than to take the money.[6] (We return to the relationship between the ability to pay and worth in chapter 4.) But economists are so accustomed to equating the worth of a good to a person with how much that person can afford to pay for it that Martin Feldstein could make this equation the pivotal element of his American Economic Association presidential address. The two are not the same, and this is precisely why insurance exists: to let people see the doctor when they cannot afford to.

Currently an employer who provides health insurance to her employees may deduct the premium payments from the company's income for tax purposes. Feldstein wants to disallow this deduction to make health insurance more expensive. When insurance becomes more expensive to employers, Feldstein explains, poor employees will be forced to settle for higher deductibles and higher co-pays, and they will use less medical care. If Feldstein's advice is followed, the poor will pay with their lives, because increases in co-pays lead patients to forgo immunization, cancer screening, and lifesaving drugs.[7]

FIGURE 3.2: MARTIN FELDSTEIN, 1939–

"[Low co-payments] lead to an increased demand for care that is worth less than its cost of production."

Credit: Alex Wong/Getty Images

Needless to say, according to Feldstein, while medical care for the poor may be worth less than its cost, this does not hold for the rich. To continue our example, let's suppose that the reservation price of Rich for a doctor's visit is $100.01. The insurance company would have to pay her this sum or more for skipping the visit, but the doctor's fee is less than that. In other words, a low co-payment rate for the rich would be Pareto efficient because the rich don't really need it.

The Utilitarian View

A utilitarian would first note that health insurance is a redistributive policy that transfers money from people who are healthy to people who are sick. People buy health insurance because they want the ability to get medical care when they need it; to a Utilitarian the claim that getting medical care that one could not personally afford is inefficient would be strange.

Does tax-subsidized health insurance increase the sum of utilities in society? Nothing gives greater utility to people than their health. The gain in utility to a patient who visits the doctor probably exceeds the loss in utility to those who pay for it. Nevertheless, not all employers provide health insurance, and among those that do there is a great variation in the level of benefits. This means that the tax deductibility of insurance premiums is not equitable. Rather than cancelling the deductions, however, it may be better to require all employers to provide a uniform insurance policy.

IT IS NOT PARETO EFFICIENT:
THE POOR BREATHE TOO MUCH CLEAN AIR

First World environmentalists and First World workers both have deep concerns about pollution in the Third World. The environmentalists worry that the Third World cannot afford to say no to polluting factories; the workers worry that because of lax environmental regulations in the Third World, factories will move there, taking their jobs with them. Lawrence Summers, who we have already encountered and who would eventually become President Clinton's treasury secretary and President Obama's chief economic adviser, was the chief economist of the World Bank from 1991 to 1993. His position regarding pollution in the Third World? In a now-infamous 1991 internal memo he wrote, "I think the economic logic behind dumping a load of toxic waste in the lowest wage country is impeccable and we should face up to that."[8]

When the memo was leaked, Summers claimed that it was meant to be ironic. But tellingly, he did not say that his statement was wrong. Using Pareto efficiency as a yardstick, the economic logic is exactly as Summers described it. It is Pareto inefficient for people of the Third World to breathe clean air, because if they had to pay for it, they would not be able to afford it.

When Larry Summers made the economic case for dumping toxic waste on the Third World, it was in response to a demand by environmentalists and labor unions that the same environmental standards be applied in the Third World as in the First. What these do-gooders did not understand is that it would be Pareto inefficient to enforce in the Third World the same environmental regulations as in the First. For example, suppose that saving one life through pollution control technology costs $4 million. If the value of life in the First World is $5 million, then the $4 million should be spent and that life should be saved. But if in the Third World the value of life is only $1 million, then saving it will be Pareto inefficient, because the residents of the Third World would be better off with the additional death and a payment of, say, $2 million.[9]

Those who do not subscribe to the logic of Pareto efficiency do so at their own peril. In 1992 Brazil's Secretary of the Environment, José Lutzenberger, wrote to Summers about the American's pro-pollution remarks: "Your reasoning is perfectly logical but totally insane. . . . Your thoughts [provide] a concrete example of the unbelievable alienation, reductionist thinking, social ruthlessness, and the arrogant ignorance of many conventional 'economists' concerning the nature of the world we live in. If the World Bank keeps you as vice president it will lose all credibility. To me it would confirm what I often said . . . the best thing that could happen would be for the Bank to disappear." [10] Lutzenberger lost his job shortly after writing this letter.

The Utilitarian View

Environmental protection is often thought of as a luxury policy that only the rich can afford; this is also the assumption behind Summers's remark. But in fact, when it is enacted and enforced by a central government, environmental protection is a redistributive policy, and it is necessary not because a given First World country is rich, but because some communities within that country are poor. If these communities had to choose between jobs in polluting factories on the one hand and a clean environment on the other, they would choose the former. When environmental standards are set and enforced by the central government, however, workers cannot negotiate their health away. Thus, when it is enforced uniformly, environmental protection has the greatest beneficial impact in the poorest communities.

Environmental protection takes money from factory owners, who are forced to invest in clean technologies, and from consumers, who end up paying higher prices, and transfers it to poor communities in the form of a cleaner environment. If the gain in utility from the cleaner environment exceeds the loss in utility from the smaller profits and higher consumer prices, then environmental protection is Utilitarian efficient.

Owners who move their factories to foreign countries to avoid environmental protection in their own country end up eviscerating this protection. As more and more workers lose their jobs, public support for environmental protection will wane. Environmental protection cannot work unless all communities, local and international, are subject to it. Summers's advocacy of low environmental standards in the Third World is a prescription for low environmental standards everywhere.

If poor countries were to enforce the same environmental standards as countries in the First World do or if First World Countries started banning goods that are not produced under these same standards, some factories would return to the First World. But poor people in poor countries need protection against environmental degradation just as much as poor people in rich countries do. In China, for example, four hundred thousand people die prematurely every year because of pollution.[11] And if, in response to the loss of jobs, First World countries end up loosening their own environmental standards, workers everywhere will see the quality of the environment deteriorate, with no gains in jobs anywhere.

4

WHY REDISTRIBUTING GOODS MAY BE
PARETO EFFICIENT AFTER ALL

Economists object to the redistribution of goods because giving poor people goods that they cannot otherwise afford is Pareto inefficient. Given the utility that the poor gain from the redistribution of goods, this is a feeble objection. It turns out, however, that the claim of Pareto inefficiency is in many cases itself wrong.

The claim that the redistribution of goods is not Pareto efficient rests on the assumption that the rich have higher reservation prices for those goods than the poor do. This is a good assumption when answering one sort of question: Both Rich and Poor want to rent the same apartment. Who will get it? Rich, of course. But it is a bad assumption when answering another sort of question: Poor lives in a rent-controlled apartment that Rich covets, and subletting is legal. Will Poor sublet the apartment to Rich? The answer is, not necessarily. The reservation price of Poor, who lives in the apartment, may be higher than the reservation price of Rich, who doesn't.

Researchers discovered that when consumers are presented with the possibility of selling a good that they did not plan on selling, the price that they demand for it is on average seven times higher than the price that they themselves would have agreed to pay for it had they been in the market to buy it. The price that a person is willing to pay for a good she does not have is called the Willingness to Pay price, or WTP. The price that this same person would demand in order to sell the good once she possesses it is called the Willingness to Accept price, or WTA.

Measuring the difference between WTP and WTA is nearly impossible. At any particular moment a consumer either buys a good or sells it, but she does not sell and buy the good at the same time. When she buys, she reveals something about her WTP (that it exceeds or is equal to the price she pays) and when she sells she reveals something about her WTA (that it is less than or is equal to the price she charges), but what is not observable are both values simultaneously. The economists who estimate these values rely therefore on artificial experiments, and the results show a great variation in the ratio of WTA to WTP, from 1:1 to 1:113.[1] But most of the results are in the lower end of this spectrum, and this is why the average is 1:7. The ratio between WTA and WTP for food, health care, and housing is probably higher than for most other goods, but no measurements for these particular goods exist.[2]

Let's return to our rent control example. In the example, family G's reservation price for an apartment is $1,500/month, while family A's reservation price for the same apartment is $6,000/month. Suppose that the legal rent is no more than $500/month, and that family G lives in the apartment. Suppose also that family A makes family G the highest offer that it is able to make, $6,000/month, for the apartment. Will family G accept? Not necessarily. First, because it pays for the apartment only $500/month instead of $1,500/month, family G already has a consumer surplus of $1,000/month. In addition, the apartment is in a desirable location and the family put down roots in the neighborhood. Given the low rent, family G may choose to stay in the apartment despite A's offer. This does not mean that family G will not agree to move out for any sum, no matter how high, but it does mean that once it possesses the apartment, family G's reservation price for it is higher than family A's. There-fore, rent control may produce a Pareto efficient allocation even when it is the poorest family who ends up with an apartment as a result. The economist's objections to rent control may not be justified even accord-ing to his own yardstick.

But if the free market and rent control both produce Pareto efficient allocations, how should the government choose between them? Once again, Pareto efficiency fails to provide a tool for making public policy.

WHAT IS "JUST COMPENSATION"?

A Supreme Court decision in 2005, *Kelo v. City of New London*, shocked many Americans. Although this is not the terminology that they used, the separate dissents in this case, by Justices Sandra Day O'Connor and Clarence Thomas, were based on Utilitarian efficiency.

The events that led to the case began when executives at Pfizer, the pharmaceutical giant, decided they wanted to open a research facility in the town of New London, Connecticut. In fulfilling what has been re-ported as a condition for Pfizer's coming to town, the city of New Lon-don moved to clear the waterfront neighborhood of Fort Trumbull of its 115 residents.[3] Although 106 owners agreed to sell their properties for the price that the city government offered, 9 refused. The city then tried to use its power of eminent domain to force the 9 residents to vacate their homes and to pay them "just compensation." When they received evic-tion notices, however, instead of taking the money and leaving, the resi-dents took their case to the Supreme Court.

Both dissents addressed the magnitude of "just compensation," and news analyses described their opinions as similar. Thomas even signed O'Connor's decision. But in fact the decisions reflected very different, al-most opposite, views.

Thomas disagreed that the residents *could* be justly compensated, explaining that "so-called 'urban renewal' programs provide some compensation for the properties they take, but no compensation is possible for the subjective value of these lands to the individuals displaced." Thomas obviously exaggerated. Even he could not possibly believe that "no compensation is possible." But when a government needs land for a project, it often chooses to condemn the homes of the poor and not of the rich, because it believes that the "just compensation" will be lower. Thomas searched for an argument that would counter this logic. He wanted to explain why the value of a home to a poor family is *not* lower than the value of a home to a rich family, even if the sale prices of the homes themselves are different. One reason Thomas may have claimed that the value of a home to its inhabitants is infinite is because infinity is the same for the poor as it is for the rich. While the value of a home is not in fact infinite, it can still have the same value, or an even higher value, for the poor family than for the rich, if this value is measured not in dollars but in utility. The reason is that the rich family has greater means to adjust to the loss of its home. Thus for a poor family WTA may be higher than it is for a rich family. Because he implicitly compared the utility of the poor to the utility of the rich, the test that Thomas used was that of Utilitarianism.

Justice O'Connor also raised the issue of "just compensation," and she did it through the case of one plaintiff, Wilhelmina Dery, who was born in 1918 in the house where she was still living with her husband of sixty years. The home of Mrs. Dery had been in her family for one hundred years, and the Derys' son lived next door to them. Clearly, being evicted would cause them pain. A house acquires extra value to the family that occupies it, well above the market price, and O'Connor believed that paying the owners of the taken property the market value of their property would not compensate them sufficiently for their losses. While O'Connor was no doubt correct, a consistent application of her argument only buttresses the practice of giving larger compensation to wealthier property owners when their property is taken. O'Connor was concerned with the value of what was taken while Thomas was concerned with people's capacity to adjust to the taking.

The state of Michigan responded to the New London decision with a new law, which addresses O'Connor's concerns, not Thomas's. The law requires that the "just compensation" for a primary residence be no less than 125 percent of the market price.[4] This strengthens even further the incentive of the government to take the property of the poor and not of the rich, a remedy to the *Kelo* decision that is clearly not Utilitarian.

The preferential treatment that the rich get from the government came into sharp focus with the compensation for the families of the victims of the 9/11 attack. Wealthy families received substantially higher compensations than poor families did, even though the former were better equipped to absorb the loss than the latter. It is clear that what's missing is a principle that would govern the redistribution of income by the government. Without it, the government spends taxes to shore up the existing distribution of income, no matter how unequal it is.

THE PIE OF TAXES

In the United States today, several programs deliberately transfer money from the rich to the poor, including welfare, governmental health services, and public housing and housing subsidies. But the most significant transfer of money from the rich to the poor occurs not deliberately but as a by-product of the provision of governmental services financed by taxes.

As an example, suppose that there are two families, one with an annual income of $30,000, and one with an annual income of $300,000. Assume also that there is no education provided by the government and that each family has one child that it sends to a private school at a cost of $15,000/year. The ratio between the families' after-tuition incomes is 19:1 ($285,000/$15,000). If public education were established, then the government would have to collect a tax from these two families to pay for it. If the income tax were progressive, the rich family would certainly end up subsidizing the poor one. But even if the tax rate were flat, money would be redistributed from the rich to the poor. A rate of 9.1 percent would be needed to generate the required $30,000. With this rate the poor family would see its payment for education decrease from $15,000 to $2,727, while the payment of the rich family would increase to $27,273. The ratio between the after-tax incomes of these families would then be only 10:1 (the after-tax income of the rich family would be $272,727 and of the poor family $27,272). Thus even a regressive tax, such as a sales tax, is redistributive, as long as the rich pay more of it in absolute terms and the tax is used to provide the same goods and services for rich and poor.

5

A BRIEF HISTORY OF THE FEDERAL INCOME TAX

In 1787 the Founding Fathers incorporated into the Constitution a clause that forbade the establishment of an income tax. Article 1 of the Constitution read, "No capitation, or other direct, Tax shall be laid, unless in Proportion to the Census or Enumeration herein before directed to be taken." In other words, Congress was entitled to levy a constant tax per person, a "poll tax," but not a tax that is proportional to income and therefore takes more money from the rich than from the poor.

While we don't know why the Founding Fathers specifically opposed the income tax, Thomas Jefferson believed that redistribution would violate some "first principle":

> To take from one, because it is thought his own industry and that of his father has acquired too much, in order to spare to others who (or whose fathers) have not exercised equal industry and skill, is to violate arbitrarily the first principle of association, "to guarantee to everyone a free exercise of his industry and the fruits acquired by it." [1]

Other Founding Fathers may have held similar views.

The Founding Fathers succeeded in delaying the income tax, but they did not succeed in preventing it. In 1913 the Constitution was modified by the Sixteenth Amendment, which explicitly permitted it: "The Congress shall have power to lay and collect taxes on incomes, from whatever sources derived, without apportionment among the several States, and without regard to any census or enumeration." And as table 5.1 makes clear, Americans did not hesitate to implement it. The income tax was levied just as soon as it became legal, and it has been used not only to finance the provision of public goods but also to expand the role of government.

TABLE 5.1: HIGHEST MARGINAL TAX RATE

Year	Top Marginal Rate	Year	Top Marginal Rate	Year	Top Marginal Rate
1913	7.0%	1931	25.0%	1949	82.13%
1914	7.0%	1932	63.0%	1950	91.00%
1915	7.0%	1933	63.0%	1951	91.00%
1916	15.0%	1934	63.0%	1952	92.00%
1917	67.0%	1935	63.0%	1953	92.00%
1918	77.0%	1936	79.0%	1954	91.00%
1919	73.0%	1937	79.0%	1955	91.00%
1920	73.0%	1938	79.0%	1956	91.00%
1921	73.0%	1939	79.0%	1957	91.00%
1922	56.0%	1940	81.10%	1958	91.00%
1923	56.0%	1941	81.00%	1959	91.00%
1924	46.0%	1942	88.00%	1960	91.00%
1925	25.0%	1943	88.00%	1961	91.00%
1926	25.0%	1944	94.00%	1962	91.00%
1927	25.0%	1945	94.00%	1963	91.00%
1928	25.0%	1946	86.45%	1964	77.00%
1929	24.0%	1947	86.45%	1965	70.00%
1930	25.0%	1948	82.13%	1966	70.00%

1967	70.00%	1982	50.00%	1997	39.60%
1968	75.25%	1983	50.00%	1998	39.60%
1969	77.00%	1984	50.00%	1999	39.60%
1970	71.75%	1985	50.00%	2000	39.60%
1971	70.00%	1986	50.00%	2001	38.60%
1972	70.00%	1987	38.50%	2002	38.60%
1973	70.00%	1988	28.00%	2003	35.00%
1974	70.00%	1989	28.00%	2004	35.00%
1975	70.00%	1990	31.00%	2005	35.00%
1976	70.00%	1991	31.00%	2006	35.00%
1977	70.00%	1992	31.00%	2007	35.00%
1978	70.00%	1993	39.60%	2008	35.00%
1979	70.00%	1994	39.60%	2009	35.00%
1980	70.00%	1995	39.60%	2010	35.00%
1981	69.13%	1996	39.60%		

Source: Eugene Steuerle and Joseph Pechman, Joint Committee on Taxation, Summary of Conference Agreement on the Jobs and Tax Relief Reconciliation Act of 2003, JCX-54-03, May 22, 2003; IRS Revised Tax Schedule[2]

As the tax rates in table 5.1 show, in 1917, just four years after the change in the Constitution that permitted the income tax, the highest tax bracket was set at 67 percent when the United States entered World War I, and a year later it was raised to 77 percent. In 1925 the top rate was cut to 25 percent, but this low rate lasted for only a short period. The Depression started in 1929, and the government launched programs that required a great deal of money. It hired workers directly in order to provide them with jobs, and the Social Security and the Aid for Families with Dependent Children programs were created. In 1932 the top rate was raised to 63 percent, and it stayed above 60 percent until 1982, a period of fifty years. There was then even a period of fourteen years, from 1950 to 1964, during which it was above 90 percent. What turned Americans against the government and against taxes? Whatever the answer may be, economists played an active role in facilitating the break with the past. How? According to these economists, high taxes are Pareto inefficient. Because no threshold between low and high taxes was specified, in practice any tax rate has been deemed too high.

6.

IT IS NOT PARETO EFFICIENT: THE RICH PAY TOO MUCH TAXES (OR, LAFFER'S NAPKIN)

In 1974 Arthur Laffer, an economist at the University of Chicago, traveled to Washington to meet with Donald Rumsfeld, President Gerald Ford's chief of staff. Laffer had a new theory about why the top tax rate was inefficiently high, and *Wall Street Journal* writer Jude Wanniski prevailed on Rumsfeld to meet with him. But at the last minute Rumsfeld decided not to attend the meeting himself, and to take it out of the White House. His deputy, Dick Cheney, went to the meeting instead, which took place in a bar. There, on a napkin, Laffer drew a diagram that showed why taxing the rich "too much" is bad for the country. Neither Rumsfeld nor Cheney acted on Laffer's theory[1] President Ford did not propose cutting taxes, and the top marginal tax rate remained at 70 percent throughout his presidency. Things changed, however, when the napkin fell into the hands of President Reagan in 1981.

A version of Laffer's diagram is shown in Figure 6.1. The napkin itself did not survive, and now any curve that shows that increasing the tax rate beyond a threshold causes tax revenues to decrease is called a Laffer Curve. In our depiction the Maximum Revenue Tax Rate—the tax rate at which the most tax dollars will be collected—is drawn at a 50 percent rate, but this is entirely arbitrary. As will be shown below, the actual rate must be close to 100 percent. It was the Laffer Curve that was used to justify Ronald Reagan's drastic cuts in taxes.

Why would a higher tax rate cause revenues to *decrease* according to Laffer? Because it would cause the rich to cut the hours that they work, and when they earn less they pay less in taxes. (The argument does not apply to poor workers because when their taxes are raised they must work *harder* in order to meet their basic needs.) In Laffer's view, with a lower tax rate there would be more tax money, and that means that a high tax rate is Pareto inefficient.

One particularly clever aspect of Laffer's theory is that it parts from our normal understanding of the relationship between taxes and government expenditure. He claimed that the government would collect more taxes at a lower tax rate, making it possible to appear to be pro-government and anti-taxes at the same time.

Would tax collection really increase if the top tax rate were decreased? This is an empirical question, and we examine the evidence below. But no one could truly have believed that the deep tax cuts passed during the

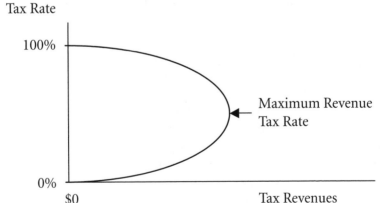

FIGURE 6.1: THE LAFFER CURVE

FIGURE 6.2: ARTHUR LAFFER, 1940–

Source: AP Images

Reagan years would increase tax revenues. From 1981 to 1988 the top rate decreased from 50 percent to 28 percent.[2] Suppose that a wealthy individual works sixty hours a week, forty of which go into her earning the $1 million that is subject to the top tax bracket.[3] When the top tax rate is 50 percent, the government collects $500,000 in taxes on this $1 million. For the government to collect the same $500,000 from this individual with a tax rate of 28 percent, this individual would have to earn $1.8 million in the top bracket, or she would have to work thirty-one *additional* hours a week. In other words, justifying the 1980s tax cuts by the Laffer Curve was a ruse.

Martin Feldstein, whom we have already encountered, became

Reagan's chair of the Council of Economic Advisers in 1982; it was on his watch that the Reagan tax cuts took effect. Nevertheless, in a 1986 article Feldstein divulged that he never believed Laffer: "The height of supply side hyperbole was the 'Laffer curve' proposition that the tax cut would actually increase tax revenue because it would unleash enormously depressed supply of effort." [4] But this was kept top secret. In 1981 President Reagan promised that his tax and spending cuts would spur the economy to grow at almost 5 percent a year. [5] Feldstein did not oppose the tax cuts either before he assumed office or after.

The evidence that was collected after the tax cuts showed what the

FIGURE 6.3: PRESIDENT REAGAN MEETS THE PRESS ABOUT THE ECONOMIC RECOVERY TAX ACT, CALIFORNIA, 1981

"Government is not the solution. Government is the problem."

Source: Photo courtesy the Ronald Reagan Library

chair of the Board of Economic Advisers knew when he collaborated in their implementation. All three of Reagan's claims were wrong. The increase in the work effort of the rich after the tax cuts was minuscule:[6] as table 6.1 shows, tax revenues grew at a robust rate of 2 percent in the years 1948–79, when the highest tax rate ranged from 70 percent to 91 percent, while their growth rate declined to 0 percent in the following ten years; the economy also grew faster in the high tax years than it did in the low tax years.[7] In the 1990s taxes were raised somewhat, and not surprisingly revenues increased as well.

TABLE 6.1: ECONOMIC AND REVENUE GROWTH: SELECTED PERIODS

(All economic and revenue figures are expressed as average annual growth rates, adjusted for inflation and population growth, i.e., average per-person growth rates.)

FISCAL YEARS	GROWTH OF GDP	GROWTH OF INCOME TAX RECEIPTS
1948–79	2.4%	1.8%
1979–90	2.0%	0.2%
1990–2000	2.0%	4.2%
2000–2015 [iii]	2.0%	0.1%

Source: Richard Kogan, "The Simple Story: Tax Cuts Lose Revenues," Center for Budget and Policy Priorities, 2004, http://www.cbpp.org/1-25-05bud2.htm

WHO PAID FOR THE LAFFER CURVE

With tax revenues growing at slower rate than the GDP in the 1980s, the federal government set out to cut its expenses. No doubt at the behest of Feldstein, the first step was to cut programs that were not Pareto efficient. Children were removed from the free school lunch program,[8] the availability of public housing and housing subsidies were severely cut,[9] and the share of the federal government in financing education was decreased from 12 percent to 6 percent (the balance is paid for by state and local governments).[10] (Disabled people were also removed from the Social Security rolls, although disability payments are actually Pareto efficient.)[11] Government spending for civilian purposes, excluding Social Security and Medicare, declined by 20 percent, from 9.3 percent of the GNP to 7.4 percent, because, as Reagan was fond of saying, "government is not the solution, government is the problem."[12]

In addition, with federal tax revenue so far behind the growth of GDP, many responsibilities of the federal government were transferred to state and local governments, and they, unwilling to raise their own taxes, have responded by cutting services and shedding responsibilities entirely.

The poorest citizens have been the hardest hit. With welfare reform, welfare became a local responsibility, and in New York City, for example, this meant that in the years 2001–6 the number of people receiving public assistance decreased by 103,000 while the number of poor individuals increased by 60,000 (52,000 adults, 8,000 children).[13] Nationally, states diverted welfare block grants to other programs, in effect stealing from the poor to finance their budgets.[14] But the poorest citizens are not the only ones paying for the lower federal taxes. In New York City tuition for the City University of New York four-year colleges increased 37 percent in 1992, 32 percent in 1993, 31 percent in 1996, and 25 percent in 2004, for a cumulative increase of 96 percent over a twelve-year period.[15] Nationally, tuition in state universities increased 472 percent over the years 1981–2005.[16] Median personal income increased by 132 percent over the same period, less than one-third of the increase in tuition. (In private universities, tuition increased by 419 percent.)[17]

While the federal government has been shifting its responsibilities to lower levels of government, with no lower levels under them, local governments have been shifting their responsibilities to the private sphere.

City governments across the country now provide packages of services and taxes in the form of Business Improvement Districts, which are tailored to the means of the neighborhoods that finance them, so that no subsidization of the poor by the wealthy occurs. The wealthier the neighborhood the cleaner and safer the streets; in the wealthiest neighborhoods, the Business Improvement Districts replace the unsightly city-issued garbage cans, add stylish lighting, and assign friendly security guards to patrol the streets. Not surprisingly, a recent study discovered that in Los Angeles crime rates are lower in neighborhoods that have formed Business Improvement Districts.[18] In New York City the parks are also private now. Wealthy neighborhoods finance the maintenance of "their" parks and nobody else's. And let's not forget the ambulance system in New York. It used to be public, but it is now "enhanced" by ambulances of the private hospitals, with the result that in wealthy neighborhoods ambulances became ubiquitous, ready to take insured and paying patients to private hospitals and uninsured and nonpaying patients to public hospitals, regardless of which hospital is nearest. Poor neighborhoods are left to rely on the public ambulance system and on public hospitals that now have far fewer paying patients.[19]

BECAUSE OF HIGH TAXES THE RICH CONSUME PERKS

After almost thirty years the Reagan tax cuts are still with us, but President Obama threatens to abolish them after the current recession ends. The opponents of redistribution have been preparing new ammunition against higher taxes for just such a moment. The data that showed that lower tax rates do not encourage the rich to work harder had just been published when Martin Feldstein came up with yet another reason why high tax rates are bad for "the economy." According to him, in the pre-Reagan years, when the tax rates were high, company executives avoided paying taxes by taking their pay in the form of "perks" instead of wages.[20] These perks are often extremely costly to shareholders. They include corporate jets, special dining rooms, special health treatments, designer shower curtains, and birthday extravaganzas for CEOs' wives. According to economists these perks are Pareto inefficient because executives don't really want them. A corporate jet costs many millions of dollars, and according to economists CEOs would gladly trade them in for much lower payments in cash. Feldstein contends that because tax rates are now lower, CEOs are not averse to high salaries, and as a result, the consumption of executive perks is lower.

You might think that Feldstein would present data about the consumption of perks before and after Reagan's tax cuts to support his theory, but he doesn't. What he considers evidence that management's consumption of perks decreased is the fact that after the tax cut income inequality in the United States has increased. Feldstein's logic would have been valid if the only way for executives to increase their compensation was to reduce their consumption of perks. But in real life, executives can increase both their compensation *and* their consumption of perks at the same time. Until 2005, companies could hide these perks by classifying them simply as business expenses. But a change in reporting requirements by the Securities and Exchange Commission has lifted the veil, which led *BusinessWeek* to run a story titled, "Exec Perks: An Ugly Picture Emerges."[21] The disclosures only confirmed what most suspected anyway. Even with lower taxes and higher income, executives were given everything from corporate jets for personal use to membership in country clubs even *after* they retire. Between 1991 and 2002 the number of companies that owned corporate jets, instead of decreasing, as Feldstein claimed would surely happen, increased by fifty-five.[22] The *New York Times* reported in 2007 that in Oregon there is a golf course that is the destination of five thousand corporate jets annually. (An airport that serves the golf course almost exclusively has been built and is maintained by taxpayers and the general flying public.)[23] Feldstein was correct, though, about the increase in inequality. Between 1990 and 2004 executive "compensation," measured in workers' wages, increased fourfold (figure 6.4). Even if the consumption of perks had vanished altogether, it could not account for more than a tiny fraction of this change.

FIGURE 6.4: AVERAGE EXECUTIVE TO AVERAGE PRODUCTION WORKER PAY RATIO, 1990–2005

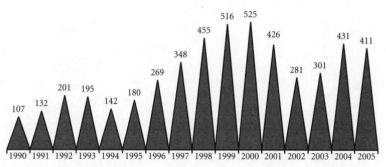

Source: Sarah Anderson and John Cavanagh (Institute for Policy Studies), Scott Klinger and Liz Stanton (United for a Fair Economy), "Executive Excess 1990–2005"

With only 48 guests
on a plane built for 220, everything changes...

Introducing Eos,
The Commercial Corporate Jet™

THE PIE OF THINGS

Inequality is not simply a description of how the pie of things is divided. It is also a force that determines how big the pie is. In the following two chapters we will see that inequality itself causes the pie of things to be smaller.

Chapter 7 deals with goods that are supplied in the private market. It shows that because of inequality, rock stars are better off performing in front of small audiences in private parties instead of large crowds in public venues; real estate developers are better off building a small number of fantastically large apartments instead of a large number of apartments of normal size; airlines are better off providing just a handful of passengers full-length beds instead of providing all passengers adequate legroom; doctors are better off seeing a small number of patients for extra-long visits, instead of seeing a larger number of patients who otherwise can only see the nurse; and drug manufacturers are better off keeping the supply of life-saving drugs low even if this means that millions of people die.

Chapter 8 deals with goods and services that are provided by the government and focuses on a service that is central to our quality of life, education. It shows that because of inequality the overall quality of public education is low and the disparity in the funding of public education across school districts is large.

Inequality makes the pie of things smaller, yet economists measure the size of the pie not by how much substance it contains but by its price. It is entirely possible, therefore, for economists to measure as growth what most people experience as economic decline.

7.

PRIVATE GOODS

MONOPOLIES

We have been taught to think of monopolies as bad for consumers. As the Parker Brothers game seems to demonstrate, she who monopolizes most markets ends up with the most money. But monopolies themselves are not inherently bad. A monopolist often comes to be either because costs are minimized when all consumers use the same product or because the monopolist produces the best product and consumers prefer it to all others. Nevertheless, monopolists are antisocial: they charge prices that are too high, thus excluding poorer consumers.

As this section shows, monopolies are ubiquitous, and the problem therefore cannot be ignored. Furthermore, the consumers excluded by the high prices that monopolies charge are not only the poor but also the middle class. Nevertheless, regulating the price that each monopoly charges is not a practical solution; there are simply too many of them. The high price that a monopolist charges is due not only to its monopoly power, however, which in itself is a positive thing, but because it faces customers with an unequal distribution of income. Reducing inequality, difficult as it may be, is perhaps the most practical solution to the problem of monopolies.

A Monopolist Charges Too Much and Sells Too Little

In order to analyze the behavior of a monopolist, let's consider a highly stylized example of the market for breakfast cereal. Let's assume that the cost of producing one box of cereal is $1.00, and that manufacturers normally earn a markup of one-half of cost, which in our case comes to 50¢. Let assume also that table 7.1 represents the reservation prices of consumers, and that each consumer needs exactly one box. Given these reservation prices, what will be the price of a box of cereal and how many units will be sold altogether?

TABLE 7.1: RESERVATION PRICES FOR BREAKFAST CEREAL

Consumer	A	B	C	D	E	F	G	H	I
Reservation Price	$5.00	$4.50	$4.00	$3.50	$3.00	$2.50	$2.00	$1.50	$1.00

We consider first the case in which the market is competitive. The market for a good is competitive if at any moment there is at least one seller who is willing to sell as many units of the good as she can, for a price that covers the cost of production plus the normal markup. Under these conditions the market price would be $1.50/box and either seven or eight units would be purchased, depending on what buyer H, who is indifferent between buying and not buying, decides to do.

Suppose now that there is only one seller in the market. What price would the monopolist charge and how many units would she sell? Table 7.2 shows the monopolist's calculations. If she charges $5.00/box, she will be able to sell only one box, and her profit will be $3.50. (Like any other seller, the monopolist expects to earn at least the normal markup per unit, and this is why we include the markup in the cost.) If she charges $4.50/box she will be able to sell two boxes, and her profit will be $6.00. The table shows that the highest profit is achieved when the price is set at $3.50/box and the monopolist will sell only four units. In other words, compared to the equilibrium in a competitive market, a monopolist charges a higher price and sells a smaller quantity.

TABLE 7.2: MONOPOLY IN THE BREAKFAST CEREAL MARKET

CONSUMER	A	B	C	D	E	F	G	H	I
Reservation Price	5.00	4.50	4.00	3.50	3.00	2.50	2.00	1.50	1.00
Revenues	5.00	9.00	12.00	14.00	15.00	15.00	14.00	12.00	9.00
Total Cost (Including Markup)	1.50	3.00	4.50	6.00	7.50	9.00	10.50	12.00	13.50
Profit	3.50	6.00	7.50	8.00	7.50	6.00	3.50	0.00	-4.50

The monopolist's sales of cereal boxes is not Pareto efficient, however, because there is an allocation that would make at least one consumer better off without making any other consumer or the seller worse off. Under this allocation, consumers A–D continue to pay $3.50/box, but consumers E–H pay only $1.50/box. In this case nobody would be worse off but consumers E–G would be better off.

Paradoxically the Pareto inefficiency of the monopolist goes away if the monopolist is even more powerful. Suppose that the monopolist knows not only the market demand for cereal but also each person's reservation price. Then she can charge each person her own reservation price. A will pay $5.00/box, B will pay $4.50/box, and so on. In this case the profits of the monopolist are twice as large, $16.00 instead of $8.00, but because eight units would have been sold, the allocation would have been Pareto efficient.

A monopolist who is able to charge each customer a different price is called a "price-discriminating monopolist." Such a monopolist is able to transfer to herself, in the form of profit, the entire surplus that consumers would have enjoyed had the market been competitive. Yet, if the criterion for government policy is Pareto efficiency, then no action against a price-discriminating monopolist is warranted. For a Utilitarian, on the other hand, the additional power to exploit calls for more regulation, not less. We discuss the regulation of monopolies in greater detail below.

What was the source of monopoly power of the manufacturer of breakfast cereal? Presumably she "cornered" the market. But this type of monopoly is actually rare. Microsoft is the world's largest monopoly today, but it did not become a monopoly by buying out the competition. In a court case that the U.S. government brought against the software manufacturer, the government proved that Microsoft displaced Netscape as the dominant supplier of web browsers by making their Internet Explorer easier to use on the Windows operating system than the Netscape browser. The trial also made clear, however, that a dominant browser would have existed even if Microsoft had not abused its power. All that Microsoft's illegal and unfair behavior did was determine which browser would be dominant. In this case consumers are *better off* when there is a monopoly—because the same browser exists on all computers. It is not surprising, then, that eight years after Microsoft was found guilty of monopolizing the market, the market share of Internet Explorer was still 70 percent.

A monopolist emerges also when the existence of a single producer minimizes the cost of production. Take for instance the production of drugs. Testing the efficacy and safety of a drug is expensive. If a drug for a particular condition already exists, other manufacturers would be reluctant to introduce new drugs that treat exactly the same condition, since the new drug would have to be tested as well. With the market divided between two sellers each would have fewer customers, and the price of both drugs would have to be higher than the price of the single drug to cover the cost of testing each. This could set in motion a price war between the sellers until in the end only one survives.

Finally, a product also comes to dominate the market when people believe that it is better than all the rest. Lipitor, which reduces cholesterol, is the world's best-selling drug, with annual sales of close to $11 billion, but not for lack of competition.[2] Having been inundated with advertising by Pfizer, consumers now believe that Lipitor is more effective than the rest.

Of course, the reason that a monopoly *can* charge a price so high that it excludes some consumers is that the monopoly faces no competition. The reason that it would *want* to charge such a high price, however, is different. The monopolist would only want to exclude consumers when the distribution of income is unequal, and the greater the degree of inequality, the larger the number of those it would want to exclude. The breakfast cereal example can be used to illustrate this point. In table 7.3 the disparity between reservation prices is smaller, and the poorest consumer is not as poor as in table 7.2. The range of reservation prices is $2.00–$2.80 in the former, compared to a range of $1.50–$5.00 in the latter, and with the new distribution the monopolist will sell seven units instead of four, and charge $2.20/box instead of $3.50/box.

TABLE 7.3: THE BREAKFAST CEREAL MARKET WITH SMALLER INEQUALITY

CONSUMER	A	B	C	D	E	F	G	H	I
Reservation Price	$2.80	$2.70	$2.60	$2.50	$2.40	$2.30	$2.20	$2.10	$2.00
Revenues	$2.80	$5.40	$7.80	$10.00	$12.00	$13.80	$15.40	$16.80	$18.00
Total Cost (Including Markup)	$1.50	$3.00	$4.50	$6.00	$7.50	$9.00	$10.50	$12.00	$13.50
Profit	$1.30	$2.40	$3.30	$4.00	$4.50	$4.80	$4.90	$4.80	$4.50

When the difference in income between the rich and the poor is small, the monopolist has little to gain from selling only to the rich. But when the difference is large, the price that the poor can afford may be so much lower than the price that the rich can afford that the monopolist is better off ignoring the poor completely. What constitutes poor depends, of course, on the exact degree of inequality. When the rich are very rich the monopolist may sell to them exclusively, leaving out the middle class as well.

Inequality in the United States increased dramatically over the last twenty-five years. In 1979 the average American in the top 5 percent of the income distribution had 11 times the income of the average American in the bottom 20 percent; by 2000 the ratio was 19:1.[3] The consequences of the marriage of monopoly power and inequality are all around us.

In entertainment, for example, middle-class audiences must now content themselves with fewer live concerts because rock stars can now make more money charging higher prices and performing less. According to data collected by the economist Alan Krueger, over the period 1992–2003 rock stars decreased the number of shows they did by 14 percent and increased their ticket prices in such a way that despite fewer performances their revenues in real dollars increased by 20 percent. What permitted them to do so was the increase in inequality. To tap the new buying power of the rich, the stars began to price discriminate. In the beginning of the 1980s, 73 percent of rock concerts in large venues (more than 25,000 seats) charged the same price for all seats. In these venues a dedicated fan who was willing to come early could get a good seat. But by 2003 only 26 percent had this policy. And as inequality grew so did the gap between the price of the good seats and the bad ones. The price of the best seats increased the most: between the years 1996 and 2003 it has increased 10.7 percent while the lowest price ticket increased 6.7 percent.[4]

Thus middle-class audiences must now content themselves with worse seats and fewer shows.

What makes the developments in the entertainment industry particularly interesting is that it is not even certain that the stars perform less; it is possible that they actually give more performances, but for fewer and richer people. In 2005 the Rolling Stones did private birthday parties for an undisclosed fee said to be between $6.75 and $10 million, while Paul McCartney came really cheap, at $1 million a party. Elton John was in the middle, at $1.5 million per ninety-minute performance, and Neil Sedaka, the B-52s, Blues Traveler, and Billy Joel all did private parties for undisclosed sums.[5] Thus, unlike our analysis above, monopoly power in tandem with inequality does not necessarily lead to a lower production level. The same amount of entertainment may be produced, but the size of the audiences is reduced because the rich prefer exclusivity.

Krueger's own favorite explanation for the decreases in the number of public concerts is not the increase in income inequality but the fact that some consumers now download music freely from the Internet. The stars are compensating for the loss in CD sales by performing less and charging more. But the impact of fewer CD sales on the frequency of performances is in itself determined by income distribution. David Bowie, for instance, thought that he would have to perform *more* to make up for lost income: "You'd better be prepared for doing a lot of touring," he advised his fellow performers, "because that's really the only unique situation that's going to be left."[6] Bowie seems not to have realized that with increasing inequality he could make up the loss of income not by *performing* more, but by *charging* more.

As was discussed earlier, the combination of inequality and monopoly in AIDS treatment has been catastrophic. The difference between the reservation prices of patients in the First and the Third World is enormous, and as a result only enough drugs to serve the First World market are manufactured. Millions of people with AIDS in the Third World are dying prematurely not because they are poor, but because they are *poorer* than people in the First World. Inequality makes the pie of goods smaller.

CAN MONOPOLIES BE CONTROLLED?

While income equality offers a long-term solution to the problem of monopoly, an interim solution is also needed. When a monopolistic situation cannot be avoided (economists call this a "natural monopoly"), economists recommend that the government force the monopolist to charge the price that would have prevailed had the market been competitive. But economic power and political power go hand in hand, and controlling the price that a monopolist charges is often impossible. For instance, no price is more justifiably set by the government than the price of drugs. Government scientists often develop these drugs, and in other cases the government finances the research that leads to the development or clinical trial of new drugs.[7] But instead of reining in the drug monopolies, the U.S. government actually works to protect these companies' high prices.

In 1998 President Nelson Mandela signed a law that would have permitted South African drug companies to produce generic versions of AIDS drugs. The law should have been recognized by the United States as being consistent with the World Trade Organization rule that permits "compulsory licensing" in national emergencies. But instead, Americans at all levels of government attacked the South African proposal. Rep. Rodney Frelinghuysen (R-NJ) was successful at getting Congress to pass a law that temporarily cut off foreign aid to South Africa; Joe Papovich, the assistant U.S. trade representative for intellectual property, declared: "We are negative toward compulsory licensing. We think companies that have the rights to new inventions should have the right to market them the way they want"; U.S. trade representative Charlene Barshefsky denied South Africa special tariff breaks on its exports to the United States; and Vice President Al Gore pressured Mandela in person when they met.[8] (When Al Gore ran for president in 2000, his support of the drug companies came to dog his campaign.)

In December 1999 President Clinton finally issued a vague statement in support of cheap drugs to the Third World. The South Africans did not implement their law, but in 2001 GlaxoSmithKline, the manufacturer of the main anti-AIDS drug, AZT, agreed to license it to a South African manufacturer, under the condition that it be sold only in South Africa and that Glaxo receive a 30 percent royalty on all sales.[9]

The plight of AIDS victims in other countries did not capture the public eye in the same way that their plight in South Africa did, and Glaxo did not yield any more than AIDS activists explicitly demanded. The U.S. government, for its own part, has done nothing further to control the monopolist, even though Glaxo is exploiting a drug that was invented by government employees (AZT was discovered by researchers at the Michigan Cancer Institute and Duke University, who received grants from the National Cancer Institute).

President George W. Bush was no better at confronting the drug companies than President Clinton was before him. Domestically, limited drug coverage was added to Medicare in 2003, but the new law requires the federal government not to negotiate down the price of drugs. The high price of drugs is part of the reason that health insurance is expensive and beyond the reach of so many Americans who are not eligible for Medicare, and that the cost of Medicare to the federal government will reach $100 billion in 2014, leaving little money in the budget for other programs.[10]

The failure to control the prices that monopolies charge is not limited to the drug industry. The government has failed to control the price of the Microsoft Windows computer operating system, even though Windows's monopoly position is not due to its superiority as a product—for many years the Mac OS operating system was considered by most to be superior—but the need of consumers to have a prevalent standard. The oil companies have been reaping record profits in the years following the invasion of Iraq, yet even in 2006, an election year, Congress failed to tax away their monopolistic profits.

In 2004 the U.S. presidential candidate Dennis Kucinich offered a solution to the drug companies' monopoly problem that can be applied to other monopolies as well. According to Kucinich, the government should step up its own involvement in drug research even further in order to make the private drug companies unnecessary. The government would place all its discoveries and inventions in the public domain and thus prevent the emergence of monopoly power. This would not prohibit either the production of drugs by pharmaceutical companies or patents—although the life span of patents may be shortened—but under these conditions the public will be less at the mercy of such companies and pricing can be controlled to benefit the greatest number of people rather than maximize profits.

In a similar manner, the government could finance the development of computer software in universities and require that the code of this software be made public. It could also import and retail gasoline, something that the government of Finland, for instance, is already doing. When an industry is naturally monopolistic and immensely important to the public's well-being, the best protection that the public has is to be the monopolist.

ZERO-SUM GAMES EVERYWHERE

Our resources are finite, and therefore when the rich take more, everybody else is left with less. For some goods, the trade-off between consumption by the rich and by the poor is not direct. If the rich buy more shoes, this does not necessarily mean fewer shoes for the poor, because the quantity of shoes produced could be increased. The production of something else might have to be reduced, but the trade-off between what the rich consume and what the poor consume is indirect. In the case of a good that has only a finite supply, however, the trade-off is direct: if the rich take more of it, everybody else is left with less. Middle-class Americans experience this direct trade-off when they fly or buy apartments, and they have begun to experience it even when they visit the doctor.

Airplanes
Passengers in the economy class of planes have very little legroom, because the seats in business and first class now turn into beds. On Singapore Airlines's new jumbo jet, Airbus A380, the beds actually stand alone, and as a result it carries only 471 passengers, whereas Air Austral carries 840 on exactly the same jet.[11] On EOS Airlines (which went out of business in 2008) middle-class passengers were not wanted altogether because EOS flights carried only 48 passengers in planes that were made for 220. Of course, if the supply of flights were infinite, how the rich fly would have been of no consequence to the other passengers. But airports can accommodate only a finite number of planes each day, and when each plane flies fewer people, fewer people can fly. EOS was not the worst offender in 2008, however, and neither is Singapore Airlines today. Corporate jets fly even fewer people and consume even more airport time than either of these airlines did, because small planes must wait a longer

time after the plane that preceded them before they can take off (the wake that large jets produce is dangerous to small jets).

Housing
Middle-class families in New York become fully aware of how poor they really are when they try to buy apartments in Manhattan. From 1995 to 2004 the average price per square foot increased from $324 to $767, an increase of 137 percent, compared to a 24 percent increase in the consumer price index over the same period. It is important to realize that the problem middle-class families face is not simply that rich families can now pay more for apartments, but that rich families now buy *larger* apartments. In other words, the problem is that the rich reduce the supply of apartments available to the middle class. This can best be explained with our example of the housing market.

Suppose that in our example families A and B become wealthier and their reservation prices become $12,000 and $10,500 respectively for the same size apartment as before. With a total supply of six apartments, the market rent would stay in the $1,500–$2,250 range just as before, and, as before, G would be the only family without an apartment. If, however, the reservation prices of A and B are now for *double*-sized apartments, it would be as if there were two additional consumers in the market, and, as the new schedule of reservation prices below shows, the rent would rise to the $3,000–$3,750 range. In addition to G, families E and F would not have apartments either.

TABLE 7.4: WHEN THE RICH GET RICHER

FAMILY	A	B	C	D	E	F	G
Reservation Price	$6,000 $6,000	$5,250	$5,250	$4,500	$3,750	$3,000	$2,250 $1,500

According to the *New York Times*, the rich want bigger apartments not because they need more space, but because other people have a lot of space. The newspaper calls it "The Battle of the Biggest." [12] A few examples illustrate this new taste. A British financier, David Martinez, bought two whole floors of the large-footprint Time Warner Center, and knocked out the floor of the upper unit to get a higher ceiling in the lower one. [13] Calvin Klein lives in an apartment that occupies three whole floors in a tower overlooking the Hudson in Chelsea, while Martha Stewart occupies two floors in the same building. [14] Swimming pools are the latest rage. At 245 E. Fifty-eight Street is an apartment building with a full gym and a swimming pool on the third floor, but the resident of the penthouse in the same building has a sixteen-by-twenty-five-feet pool all to herself. The film director Marcus Nispel, who directed the 2003 remake of *The Texas Chainsaw Massacre*, built a swimming pool right inside his five-story town house because "space in New York is something very holy," he told David Chen of the *New York Times*. He also likes to create beauty: "I love water, and I love the idea of how it contrasts with the city." The businessman Jonathan Leitersdorf recommends a swimming pool to anybody who wants to give a good party. This has been his experience with his twenty-five-by-twelve-by-six-feet swimming pool in a triplex near NYU. (Hillary Clinton, for one, is convinced. She chose his apartment for one of her fund-raisers. [15])

The hunger of the rich for space has real consequences for middle-class families and the poor. As figure 7.1 below shows, since 1995 the price of a square foot grew much faster in the largest apartments than in all the rest. Of course, the larger apartments are located in better locations and therefore command a higher price per square foot anyway. But the location factor explains only the initial difference in price between a square foot in the different apartment sizes, not the difference in the

FIGURE 7.1: INCREASE IN PRICE PER SQUARE FOOT, MANHATTAN, 1995–2004

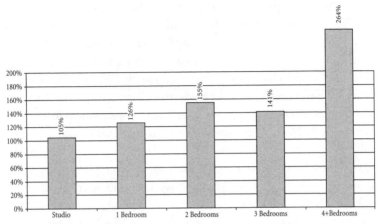

Source: Prudential Douglas Elliman Manhattan Market Report, 1995–2004

growth rates of these prices. Between 1995 and 2004, what has changed is not the view that Central Park offers, but the inequality of income.

Landlords and developers have responded to these prices as rational players would. Figure 7.2 shows that the surface area of apartments with three or more bedrooms has increased while the surface area of studios, one-bedroom, and two-bedroom apartments has decreased over that period.[16] My own calculations show that if Manhattan apartments were limited in size to 1,200 square feet, then, without constructing even one new building, the supply of apartments for ownership would increase by 35 percent, and the supply of apartments for rent would increase by 20 percent.

The increase in inequality is creating shortages in areas that were never previously associated with zero-sum games. For instance, some

FIGURE 7.2: AVERAGE SQUARE FOOTAGE BY BEDROOMS

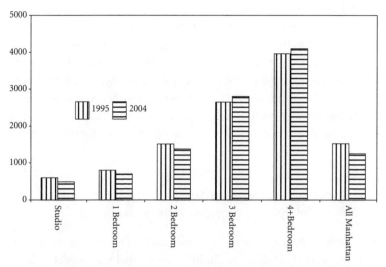

Source: Prudential Douglas Elliman, Manhattan Market Report, 1995–2004

doctors now balk at providing the same care for all patients, with the result that middle-class and poor people may soon find it difficult to see a
doctor. The phenomenon is still in its infancy, but some doctors now
charge patients an annual fee to be seen by these doctors, and in return
the doctors promise that the office visits will not be rushed and that there
won't be long waits for an appointment or in the waiting room. David
Ogden, a doctor in wealthy Marin County in California, charges "a few
hundred" patients $2,400 annually to see him. The rest of his two thou-
sand patients see only his nurse, who calls him in when she thinks she
cannot handle the case herself.[17] Doctor Jill Baron, of New York City,
wrote a letter to inform the editor of the *New York Times* that she has left
a practice where she saw many patients to open a new practice where she

sees fewer patients, and from these patients she is not accepting any health insurance.[18]

Of course, immediate appointments and more time with the doctor are both good things. But this is occurring while the number of doctors per capita is actually falling and while more doctors per capita are needed because the baby boomers are aging. It is projected that between 2000 and 2020, the number of doctors per capita will decrease by 13 percent, while between 2000 and 2035 the median age of the population will increase from 35.5 to 39.1.[19] Hence, longer doctor visits for the rich mean shorter doctor visits for everybody else.

PARETO EFFICIENCY: HOW THE PIE GETS "BIGGER" BY FEEDING FEWER PEOPLE

A few people take a lot of space on planes, and as a result many other people don't get to fly at all. A few families have palatial apartments in desirable locations, and as a result many other families can't live in these places at all. A few people have long doctor visits, and as a result many other people have to settle for seeing a nurse instead. Paradoxically, according to the way economists measure the size of the economic pie, each of these changes has made the pie of things bigger or else the change would not have taken place.

Consider, for instance, EOS Airlines. The 48 passengers on its plane paid more than what 222 passengers would have paid if the plane had only regular-sized seats. That means that the crew and the plane produced more dollars when they flew fewer people, and according to economics, that means that they were also more productive. In other words, according to economists the economic pie can become bigger simply by virtue of serving fewer people (if those people can pay more).

The fact that economists measure the size of the economic pie without regard to distribution is a direct result of their use of Pareto efficiency as the yardstick. To force a carrier like EOS Airlines to carry 222 passengers would produce an allocation of resources that is Pareto *inefficient* because *potentially* everybody could be better off when just 48 rich people fly on a plane that is intended for 222. Potentially, the rich passengers could compensate the middle-class passengers for displacing them, and the middle-class passengers could then use the money to have more doctor visits, for instance. Thus forcing EOS to fly more people would potentially make everybody worse off, which is the same as making the economic pie smaller. The problem with this argument is, of course, that in reality the compensation does not take place.

The Utilitarian View
When the distribution of income makes it Pareto efficient for a plane to transport fewer passengers and for doctors to see fewer patients, the distribution of income is itself Utilitarian inefficient. With exactly the same expenditure of resources but a more equal distribution of income, both the rich and the middle class would fly and both the rich and the middle class would see the doctor a sufficient number of times. The allocation of resources would then be both Pareto and Utilitarian efficient. Barring a redistribution of income, however, government intervention may be called for. What policies are available for the government to deal with the redistribution of goods when the redistribution of income is ruled out? We shall see that in some cases the fact that the distribution of income is unequal limits the available options.

HOW TO HANDICAP THE RICH

Doctor Visits

Should the government restrict the length of doctor visits so that more patients would be seen? Dictating to doctors how many minutes they can devote to a patient would be problematic, perhaps even immoral, and this means that in reality there is sometimes a trade-off between freedom to the rich and well-being to the poor.

Airplanes

While income inequality means more legroom in first class and less legroom in economy, as long as the number of seats on the plane is not changed it is better not to fix the problem or the middle class may not be able to travel at all. To see why, suppose that the cost of fuel for flying a two hundred-passenger plane round trip from New York to Los Angeles is $100,000. In addition suppose that the reservation price of the middle-class family for a flight is $250 and that the reservation price of a rich family for this flight, provided that it gets a large seat, is $750. A plane with only middle-class passengers would never take off because all two hundred middle-class passengers together can pay only $50,000, half the cost of the flight. The plane would be able to take off, however, with one hundred passengers who pay $750 and one hundred passengers who pay $250. Rich passengers would refuse to pay more than the middle class for the same flight, however, unless they received something extra for their money. In other words, it is the less legroom in economy and the more legroom in first class that makes it possible for the middle class to fly. What the rich gain from this arrangement is that the flights become more frequent, because without the middle class there would not be enough passengers to fill all the flights currently scheduled.

The situation is, of course, different with Singapore Airlines or corporate jets. In this case, some members of the middle class are actually prevented from flying altogether because the planes carry fewer passengers than they could. A law that would require each plane to carry its full capacity may be called for.

Housing

The simplest way to prevent rich families from living in apartments that are too large is to put a tax on space. Up to a particular threshold (which can be adjusted to family size) space would be tax-exempt. But beyond this threshold, the tax should be sufficiently high to deter excess consumption even by the very rich. To gain an appreciation of how high this tax would have to be to make a difference, recall that a square foot in a large apartment in Manhattan commands a price premium of, on average, $662. Only a tax of that magnitude will remove the incentive that developers have to build super-sized apartments.

GOVERNMENT-SUPPLIED GOODS

There are goods and services that the private market will never provide. National defense is the prime example of such goods. If a private firm tried to sell national defense to private consumers, it many not find even one customer. To see why, suppose that Jane does buy national defense but John refuses to. Once national defense is provided to Jane, John would benefit from it just as much as she would, even though he had not paid for it. National defense is therefore "non-excludable," and John may refuse to pay for it not because he objects to it, but because he prefers to get it as a "free rider" instead. Cognizant of this possibility, Jane herself would probably not buy national defense either.

Economists call a good whose consumption is non-excludable a "public good." A "public good" must be paid for by the government because too many people would not pay for it voluntarily. Unlike private firms, the government does have the ability to provide public goods because it has the power to force people to pay for them. Often a public good has yet another quality, which is that its consumption is "non-rivalrous." This means that once provided, the quality of the good does not deteriorate when the number of people it serves increases. In the case of national defense, the protection that is provided to Jane does not reduce the degree to which John is protected as well.

What other goods are public? Clean air is a public good because no one can be excluded from breathing it and because one person breathing it does not take away from the ability of another person to breathe it as well. The regulation of drugs or food are also public goods because if only safe drugs and food reach the market, no consumer can be excluded from this protection, and the protection of one consumer does not detract from the value of the protection to another consumer. Police protection is in the same category as national defense, but because this protection is over a limited area only, police protection is a "local public good." The design of a city, clean streets, and street lights are also local public goods.

But governments are not limited to providing only public goods or local public goods. One of the goods the government provides is education, yet education is excludable since it is easy to prevent a child from entering a particular school. (Which happens routinely when children from underfunded schools are prevented from attending better schools in wealthier school districts.) In addition, as we shall see below, the quality of education decreases with class size, which means that public education is not only excludable, but also rivalrous. Education is therefore a private good, and the best proof of that is that the private market also provides it, since there are private schools.

If education is a private good, then why does the government provide it? One reason may be that there is a benefit to the public at large when a person furthers her own education, and the public may be better off paying for it. For example, there is evidence that, holding the occupation, skills, and education level of a worker constant, her wage is higher when she works in a city in which the average level of educational attainment is higher.[1] There is, therefore, a benefit to the public at large when a person furthers her own education, and the public may be better off paying for it. There are also economists who claim that education is a "merit good," and by this they mean that some parents are unable to see the full benefit to their children from good education, and therefore they would under-invest in their children's education. But the main reason may be that free public education is a form of redistribution that the poor demand and insist on getting. We have seen that the first French constitution im-mediately following the revolution required free public education. The Communist Manifesto also lists "free education for all children in pub-lic schools" as one of its ten demands. In the United States, public educa-tion remains a political issue, as is clear from the "No Child Left Behind" campaign.

It must be emphasized that a private good, such as education, is still private, even when the public pays for it. In a similar manner a public good remains public even when a private firm provides it. Halliburton and Blackwater are private companies that produce national defense, but their product is nevertheless a public good because unless the public pays for it, no one else will. (In fact, it is precisely because national de-fense is a public good that Halliburton and Blackwater can deliver offen-sively poor services at astronomically high prices. An unsatisfied buyer of a private good would simply stop buying it. But because a public good is non-excludable, an individual consumer cannot simply stop consuming or paying for it.)[2]

REDISTRIBUTIVE EDUCATION

When the government provides a public good that is national, all citizens get to enjoy it equally. But when the government provides local public goods or private goods, it can and does provide different qualities and quantities to different people. For instance, as noted above, the Business Improvement Districts that city governments establish provide varying packages of taxes and services within the same city. Park conservancies funnel funds to some parks and not to others. Poor people go along with these disparities in most cases, but when it comes to education they sometimes resist, demanding that their schools be given the same amount of funds that schools in wealthier jurisdictions receive. But this demand is almost invariably met with the claim that "you cannot throw money at education." Poor schools should not receive more money because this money would simply be wasted.

Table 8.1 presents the difference in education spending between rich and poor districts in the different states. As the table shows, in some states poor districts get more funding than wealthy districts. Massachusetts spends $1,343 more per student in poor districts than in rich ones, followed by Alaska and Delaware with $1,231 and $1,184 respectively. In other states, however, rich districts get more funding than poor districts, and New York State has the largest gap between rich and poor districts, $2,040, followed by Illinois and Virginia with gaps of $2,026 and $1,105 respectively. For the country as a whole the gap is $868, which means that on average a class with twenty-five students has $21,700 more available to it to spend on specialized teachers, supplies, or trips when it is in a rich district than when it is in a poor district. Further, it is estimated that to provide the same quality of education in poor as in rich neighborhoods, spending in poor neighborhoods would have to be 40 percent higher than it is in rich neighborhoods because of a greater need for smaller class sizes there.[3]

TABLE 8.1: FUNDING GAPS IN EDUCATION BY STATE, 2001–2

STATE	2001–2002 GAP BETWEEN REVENUES AVAILABLE PER STUDENT IN THE HIGHEST- AND LOWEST-POVERTY DISTRICTS (COST-ADJUSTED DOLLARS, NO ADJUSTMENT FOR LOW-INCOME STUDENTS)
Alabama	–$613
Alaska	$1,231

Arizona	−$681
Arkansas	−$149
California	$173
Colorado	−$38
Connecticut	$277
Delaware	$1,184
Florida	−$74
Georgia	$721
Idaho	−$96
Illinois	−$2,026
Indiana	−$25
Iowa	−$333
Kansas	$122
Kentucky	−$3
Louisiana	−$725
Maine	−$79
Maryland	−$558
Massachusetts	$1,343
Michigan	−$564
Minnesota	$1,031
Mississippi	−$18
Missouri	$354
Montana	−$450
Nebraska	$233
Nevada	$333
New Hampshire	−$795
New Jersey	$1,260
New Mexico	$374
New York	−$2,040
North Carolina	−$392
North Dakota	$653
Ohio	$186

(continued)

TABLE 8.1: FUNDING GAPS IN EDUCATION BY STATE, 2001–2 *(continued)*

STATE	2001–2002 GAP BETWEEN REVENUES AVAILABLE PER STUDENT IN THE HIGHEST- AND LOWEST-POVERTY DISTRICTS (COST-ADJUSTED DOLLARS, NO ADJUSTMENT FOR LOW-INCOME STUDENTS)
Oklahoma	$226
Oregon	$186
Pennsylvania	−$882
Rhode Island	$108
South Carolina	$370
South Dakota	$552
Tennessee	$570
Texas	−$388
Utah	$782
Vermont	−$766
Virginia	$1,105
Washington	$160
West Virginia	−$135
Wisconsin	$108
Wyoming	$381
USA	−$868

Source: Education Trust Fund, http://www2.edtrust.org/NR/rdonlyres/30B3C1B3-3DA6-4809-AFB9-2DAACF11CF88/0/funding2004.pdf

Many variables combine to determine the quality of education, and one of these is class size. Figure 8.1 and figure 8.2 show class size in poor and other districts in the United States. (The first figure is for general teachers—teachers who teach all subjects—normally in lower grades. The second is for specialist teachers—teachers who teach particular topics—normally in higher grades.) In nonpoor districts 62 percent of general teachers teach in classes with eighteen or fewer students. The re-

FIGURE 8.1: CUMULATIVE CLASS SIZE IN POOR AND
OTHER SCHOOLS: GENERAL TEACHERS

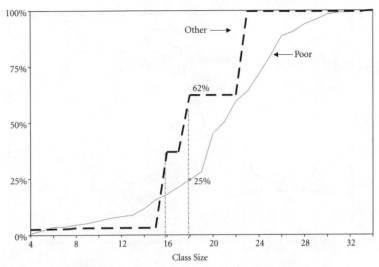

Note: A school is poor if it has any students who participate in the free school lunch program. Special education teachers and classes with more than forty-five students in classroom were excluded from the calculations.

Source: School and Staffing Survey, 1999–2000, National Center for Education Statistics (author's calculations)

spective figure in poor districts is 25 percent. The difference for specialist teachers (higher grades) is smaller, but it is still substantial. In nonpoor districts 45 percent of teachers teach in classes with seventeen or fewer students whereas in poor neighborhoods only 18 percent teach in classes of similar sizes.

But the difference in class size between nonpoor and poor public schools is dwarfed by the difference in class size between public schools and nonsectarian private schools. As table 8.2 shows, classes in such

**FIGURE 8.2: CUMULATIVE CLASS SIZE IN POOR AND
OTHER SCHOOLS, SPECIAL SUBJECT TEACHERS**

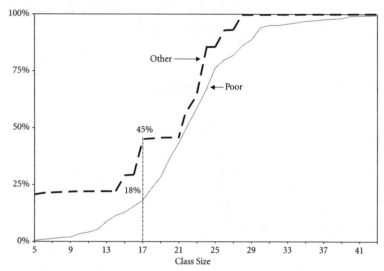

Note: A school is poor if it has any students who participate in the free school lunch program. Special education teachers and classes with more than forty-five students in the classroom were excluded from the calculations.

Source: School and Staffing Survey, 1999–2000, National Center for Education Statistics (author's calculations)

private schools are far smaller than they are in public schools, and so is the student-to-teacher ratio.

"YOU CAN'T THROW MONEY AT EDUCATION"

The inequality in funding between different school districts for education is often challenged in the courts, and when such a lawsuit takes

TABLE 8.2: AVERAGE CLASS SIZE,
STUDENT/TEACHER RATIOS, 1999–2000

	Average Class Size		Student/ Teacher Ratio	Percent of Schools with a Student/ Teacher Ratio Less Than 10:1
	Self-Contained	Departmen-talized		
Public	21	24	16:1	10%
Private Non-sectarian	15	15	9:1	68%

Source: U.S. Department of Education, NCES, Schools and Staffing Survey (SASS), "Public, Public Charter, and Private School and Teacher Surveys," 1999–2000

place, economist Eric A. Hanushek of the Hoover Institute is often there to testify that redistributing education funds would be a waste of money. In 2000, for example, North Carolina was sued by several poor school districts in Hoke County, which complained that their classes are larger and the quality of their teachers lower than in richer districts. In his testimony in this case, Hanushek told the court that there is "little systematic evidence of a correlation between spending on schools and student achievement."[4] In other words, the poor school districts may be right, but forcing the state to give them more money will not accomplish anything. Hanushek plays on the widespread belief that "the government can't do anything right." Yes, poor kids go to bad schools. Yes, these schools are underfunded. But the schools are not bad because they are underfunded. According to Hanushek and others like him, the fact that the United States spends more per capita on education than many other nations yet does not receive the same results is an argument against increasing the funding of poor schools. In an article in *USA Today* in 2004, then U.S. Secretary of Education Rod Paige repeated the mantra:

> We still have a two-tiered public education system. Some fortunate students receive a world-class education. But millions are mired in mediocrity, denied a high-quality education. Most are children of color. This is not the legacy of Brown we imagined. Some still believe we can fix our public education system by spending more money. But we already spend more per pupil on K–12 education than any other country except Switzerland. The issue is how the money is being invested.[5]

It is this mantra that permitted President Bush to call for tax cuts and education spending cuts simultaneously. As we shall see, however, the evi-

FIGURE 8.3: ERIC HANUSHEK

Credit: Photo courtesy of Eric Hanushek

dence shows that increased funding does improve the quality of schools, and the claim that it doesn't is based on a distortion of this evidence.

The claim that you can't throw money at education is backed by the observation that between 1967 and 1996 spending on education in real terms doubled, but achievement changed very little. Achievement is determined by a National Assessment of Education Progress test that is given to a sample of students periodically by the U.S. Department of Education. Figure 8.4 and Figure 8.5 show the average scores for different age groups between 1971 and 2004.[6]

At first glance the figures are alarming: the curves are flat for

FIGURE 8.4: TRENDS IN AVERAGE READING SCORES, 1971–1996

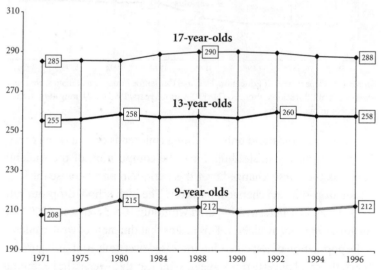

Source: U.S. Department of Education, National Center for Education Statistics, National Assessment of Education Progress (NAEP), various years, 1973–2004, long-term trend assessment in reading

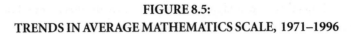

FIGURE 8.5:
TRENDS IN AVERAGE MATHEMATICS SCALE, 1971–1996

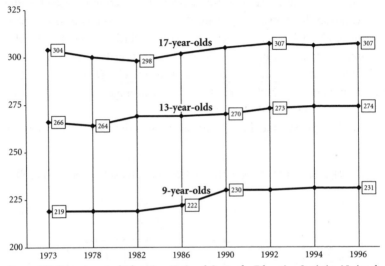

Source: U.S. Department of Education, National Center for Education Statistics, National
Assessment of Educational Progress (NAEP), various years, 1973–2004, long-term trend
assessment in mathematics

seventeen-year-olds, and only for young children is there a rising curve.
But the graphs are misleading. First, the composition of the students
who took these tests changed over this period, in part because the high
school drop-out rate changed markedly. The high school drop-out rate
in 1973 was 14.1 percent compared with only 10.9 percent in 2000 (the
rate for 1996 is not available). This means that the share of weak students
in the population of test takers has increased overtime. And, as Figure 8.6
shows, the child poverty rate was also significantly lower at the beginning
of the period than at its end. In 1973 it was 14 percent while in 1996 it was

FIGURE 8.6:

PERCENTAGE OF CHILDREN LIVING IN POVERTY, 1971–2007

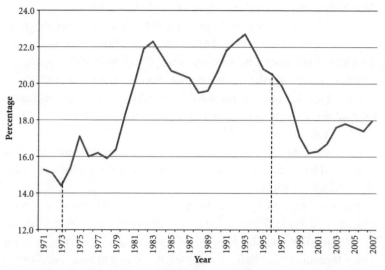

Source: U.S. Census Bureau, Historical Poverty Tables, Table 3—Poverty Status of People, by Age, Race, and Hispanic Origin (1959 to 2006)

21 percent. With a far higher component of poor children in school, one would expect average achievement rates to drop.

Also misleading is the claim that the spending per student doubled. An examination of the figures by Richard Rothstein and Karen Hawley Miles showed that the increase in per student funding from 1967 to 1991 was actually only 26 percent, not 100 percent, and that during the period 1991–96 the per student spending increased very little.[7] The disparity in the figures comes from several sources. First, the 100 percent increase in education spending figure is based on the Consumer Price Index, but the

CPI reflects what consumers buy, not what schools buy. Consumers spend a large share of their money on goods, but schools spend most of their budgets on the services of teachers and other staff members. Rothstein and Miles therefore used a price index that gives a higher weight to services. Second, Rothstein and Miles discovered that a large portion of the increase in school funding came from programs such as special education, which are worthwhile but do not affect test results (special education students, for one, are excluded from NAEP tests). The conclusion from all this information, according to Rothstein and Miles, is not that "you can't throw money at education," but that a modest increase in education spending prevented a likely *decline* in education performance that would have occurred because of increasing student poverty and declining drop-out rates.

Perhaps the most important difference between rich schools and poor schools is class size. To claim that money does not matter, Hanushek has to claim also that class size does not matter. Hanushek bases this claim on a literature survey that he has conducted. According to him, some studies show that smaller class size improves performance, but many more show that it doesn't.

The economists Alan Krueger and Diane Whitmore discovered many peculiarities in Hanushek's method of counting studies on each side of the debate. For instance, instead of counting studies, Hanushek counted estimates within studies. Hanushek reviewed 59 studies and extracted from them 277 estimates. The number of estimates in a study varied widely. Two studies included 24 estimates each, and both studies, by the same authors, were based on the same data set. Other studies provided only one estimate. As Krueger explains, Hanushek's method of counting estimates instead of studies is misleading. There is no reason to assign a greater weight to a study just because it has more estimates. (An example can illustrate Krueger's argument. Suppose an investigator wishes to find out whether calories affect weight. In addition to weight and calories, the investigator also knows the ethnicity of the subjects in her data set. The investigator may first calculate the effect of calories on weight without controlling for ethnicity, and then calculate the effect of calories on weight when controlling for ethnicity. Thus the investigator would have two different estimates of the effect of calories on weight from the same data set. Suppose now that both estimates are that calories do not affect weight. Is this equivalent to having two estimates from two different data sets that show that calories do not affect weight? Of course not. The correct interpretation of these estimates is that that particular data set shows that calories do not affect weight, and that the result does not change even when controlling for ethnicity.) Krueger and Whitmore discovered that if studies are counted instead of discovered estimates, the ratio between those that find that class size does matter versus studies that find that it does not is actually four to one.[8]

To determine whether class size matters, it is necessary to compare the achievements of students who are in classes that are very similar to each other in all respects except for class size. In other words, what needs to be similar in all classes is the composition of the students (income, immigrant status, etc.) and all other educational inputs (computer equipment, art room, etc.). The only difference between the classes should be class size. But in real life, classes that are the same in all respects except class size are impossible to find because small classes are normally in rich schools and large classes in poor ones. Researchers who do not conduct controlled experiments have no choice but to make corrections to the data to account for these other differences among classes. But the corrections are necessarily problematic. The state of Tennessee avoided all these problems by conducting a controlled experiment over the years 1985–90.

In the Tennessee study, the *only* difference between classes was size, so no corrections were necessary. Students in grades K–3 in the same school were assigned either to small (13–17 students) or regular classes (22–25 students) randomly, and the assignment of teachers to small and regular classes was random as well. In the fourth grade, all students were returned to regular classes. All students were then given the same tests. The results were that the students in the smaller classes received a percentage grade that was on average between 4 percent and 5.5 percent higher (depending on grade) than students in the regular classes. Since the maximum score on the National Assessment of Education Program tests is 500, these percentage differences translate to a 20–26 point gain. Comparing these numbers to the charts of the NAEP national results depicted above shows that these increases are larger than any improvement that occurred over a twenty-year period.[9]

Class size matters, and students in smaller classes are richer. Is the allocation of small classes to rich children efficient? If efficiency means that the students who attend the small classes are the ones who would benefit from them the most, then the answer is no. The studies that Krueger reviewed show that small class size increases the educational achievement of low-income students more than of high-income students, and of low-achieving students more than of high-achieving students. In addition, these studies show that the benefits from decreasing class size diminish as the class size decreases.[10] In other words, once a class is relatively small, making it even smaller does not help much. Therefore, shifting resources from rich students who attend small classes to poor students who attend very large classes will benefit poor students more than it will hurt rich students. Of course, it is also possible to increase funding for poor districts without reducing funding for rich districts, but this would require increasing taxes.

CAN EDUCATION BE EQUAL WHEN INCOME IS NOT?

The state of North Carolina lost the *Hoke* case. The judge listened to Hanushek carefully and thanked him for pointing out that spending money without a purpose would be a total waste. But the judge thought that the districts that sued did have a purpose for the money that they were demanding. "Only a fool would find that money does not matter in education," the judge wrote.[11]

Judges have been issuing similar decisions in many states over many years. Is spending per student equal now? Schools are funded by districts, and as income inequality increases, so does the inequality in funding. The economist Caroline Hoxby examined inequality in per-pupil spending in Massachusetts and Illinois, and she discovered that in both states the degree of inequality in education spending has increased remarkably between 1950 and 1990. Further, despite the legal challenges that should have broken the link between the value of property in a district and the funding of its school, the relation between property value and per-student spending has become *stronger* over the period.[12]

Richard Rothstein, an education columnist for the *New York Times*, reports of the ingenuity of rich parents to create funding disparity even within school districts that explicitly prohibit parents from funneling private money to schools. These parents pay teachers "appreciation fees" instead of the prohibited salary increases, hire "consultants" to teach art or music classes when they are not permitted to hire extra teachers, and build libraries and stock them with books.[13] After reviewing the evidence, Hoxby concluded, "To reduce spending inequality it would probably be more practical to reduce income inequality."

"IS IT GOOD FOR THE ECONOMY?"

"Is it good for the economy?" The question illustrates the enormous sway of economic thinking, and is also an encapsulation of all that is wrong with it. Economists know, of course, that there is really no such thing as "the economy," there are only people. Yet they have succeeded in obscuring this simple truth completely. News programs report hourly about the level of and changes in the levels of numerous stock indices. But about the quality of life of teachers, construction workers, health workers, or restaurant workers they report only very rarely. Have they more time to spend with their kids today than yesterday? And has the number of people with health insurance changed? There is little doubt that hourly reports of these indices would have spurred the government to improve them, just as reports about the stock market indices do. But the living conditions of people are not what the "economy" is or what economics is about.

Not only is "the economy" not about the people who live in it; according to economists, "the economy" actually requires human sacrifice. Food subsidies? Bad for the economy. Housing subsidies? Bad for the economy. Health insurance? Bad for the economy, too.

Yet, as recent events have demonstrated, this human sacrifice is in vain. "The economy" is a colossus whose pedestal is shaky largely because it rests on a concept of efficiency that renders practically all government programs inefficient. With an adequate supply of attractive public housing, poor people would not have borrowed money at usurious rates to buy homes that they cannot afford, and the crisis that started with "subprime mortgages" would not have been. With Social Security payments that are sufficient for workers to retire on and with free public colleges that are as attractive as private ones, ordinary workers would not be forced to "play the stock market" in order to secure their retirement or their children's college education. Without workers' money invested in stocks there would have been no need to "save Wall Street in order to save Main Street" and no excuse for bailing out bankers and banks. With government-provided health insurance, workers would have greater flexibility to move from job to job and the adjustment to changing economic conditions therefore more rapid and less painful.

The rich and those who serve them often claim that the concern with the redistribution of income is petty and unproductive. Petty, because people should not envy the well-being of others; unproductive, because even though the rich are very rich, they nevertheless take only a small portion of the social pie, and redistributing their wealth would not make a difference to the well-being of the poor.

But both claims are wrong. As the first part of this book has shown, when the distribution of income is unequal, the poor and members of the middle class suffer not because they have too little money, but because they have less money than the rich. When the income gap is large, sellers choose to set prices at levels that only the rich can afford to pay, the government betrays its obligation to serve all citizens equally, and the rich take far more than their fair share of the resources that are available only in limited supply.

To see just how wrong the claim that redistribution would not make a difference is, consider that the 2008 U.S. GDP was $47,000 per capita.[14] If income were distributed equally among all individuals, a family of four would have had resources worth $188,000/year at its disposal.[15] Instead, 13 percent of individuals in the United States belong to poor families, and for a family of four the poverty threshold is $21,027, or about one-tenth of what its income would have been if income were distributed equally.[16]

Of course, the threshold of poverty and how it is determined are what Utilitarianism is all about. According to Utilitarianism the transfer of a dollar from the rich to the poor would help the latter more than it would hurt the former; therefore, not carrying out the transfer is economically inefficient. But this means that a poverty threshold should not be determined by calculating the cost of the bare minimum of necessities that a family needs, which is the government's method for calculating it, but a number that reflects the capacity of society to provide each of its members more and better goods and services as society's productive capacity and scientific knowledge increase, because people's needs are not constant but increase with them. The threshold for redistribution according to Utilitarianism is not the bare minimum, but the average. And by this threshold the majority of American families are poor. Sixty-four percent of families have income that is below the average family income.[17]

Given how much is at stake for the rich, it is doubtful that economists will discard the concept of Pareto efficiency and become Utilitarians any time soon. But the rest of us must learn to ignore them, or we will continue to be the sheep devoured by the wolf just because Pareto could not see any reason to change this state of affairs.

Of course, economists are not only against redistributing income but also have a theory that justifies the process that creates inequality to begin with. How wages are determined is the subject of the second part of this book.

Part II

THEORIES OF WAGES

INTRODUCTION: CLASSICAL AND NEO-CLASSICAL THEORIES OF WAGES

In 2007, U.S. workers produced $95,000 worth of goods and services per worker.[1] If each of them, whether CEO or worker on the shop floor, whether in the financial industry or in agriculture, earned this wage, all families could live not only well but also in affluence. But this is, of course, not the case. Nationwide, 25 percent of workers earn wages that with full-time work put them below the poverty line.[2] In New York City, 24 percent of retail workers must rely on some form of welfare payments while they are working full-time.[3] What workers do not get, executives do. In 2007, average CEO compensation for S&P 500 CEOs was $10.5 million, 344 times the pay of the average worker.[4]

Should the government intervene to reduce wage inequality? The answer depends on what the consequences of such intervention would be, and different economists have vastly different theories about the impact. According to today's textbook theory of wages, first developed by neo-classical economist John Bates Clark (1847–1938), the free market ensures that each member of the workforce is naturally paid the value of what she has produced. Any interference will create an artificial level of remuneration that will result in lost jobs. Thus a worker who earns $25,000 per year produces $25,000 per year worth of goods. If the government were to pass a law forcing that worker's employer to pay her more, it might as well print her pink slip at the same time: no employer could pay more than $25,000 for $25,000 worth of output and expect to stay in business. The same holds also for highly paid executives, but in reverse. An executive who is paid tens of millions of dollars a year in compensation produces tens of millions of dollars per year for the company. If the government were to break the link between her "compensation" and her productivity by placing a cap on her pay, she would choose either to work in a less demanding job or work less diligently.

Logical as the neo-classical theory of wages is, the classical economist David Ricardo (1772–1823) had dismissed it even before it was put forth. Knowing what each worker produces is usually impossible, he pointed out. And from this it follows that any system based on assessing productivity is fundamentally flawed. To take a current-day example, a taxi in a metropolitan city produces a total income of $100,000 a year, of which the driver receives $25,000 and the owner of the taxi receives the rest. Did the driver produce one-quarter of the total product of the taxi? Without the taxi (means of production in some economic theories), the driver (the worker) would have produced no fares, but without the driver the taxi would have produced no fares either. Taxi and driver together produced $100,000, but how much of the total each produced is impossible to tell. How then is the income of the taxi divided between them? Adam Smith (1723–90), the world's most famous economist, explained that the division of the product between the members of the team that produced it is determined by the relative bargaining power of each member (not, as contemporary economists would have it, by an objective measure of output). When the member is a capital good, such as a taxi, the bargaining is done, of course, by its owner.

If according to modern economists the consequences of government intervention to increase pay equality would be job losses, what would they be according to the classical theory of wages? If the government were to mandate that taxi drivers be paid $101,000 a year, taxi drivers would lose their jobs. But if, instead of determining the exact pay of drivers, the government were to set a ratio between the pay of the driver and the pay of the taxi owner, the classical theory of wages predicts that the only consequence of government intervention to increase pay equality would be to increase pay equality . . . without any loss of jobs.

The following chapters trace the development of these two competing theories of wages, describe their roles in policy debates and labor conflicts, review the empirical evidence regarding their validity, and show how fundamental they are to the question of whether a market system is self-regulating. These theories mark the dividing line between the "classical" and "neo-classical" economists. David Ricardo is generally regarded as the last of the former, while John Bates Clark is the first of the latter.

9

THE CLASSICAL THEORY OF WAGES

ADAM SMITH

Adam Smith's *The Wealth of Nations*, published in 1776, is perhaps the most important economics book of all time, though a more accurate title would have included a subtitle, "The Wealth of Nations: How Did It End Up in the Hands of So Few?" According to Smith, workers in the "original state" owned all that they produced:

> The produce of labour constitutes the natural recompence or wages of labour. In that original state of things which precedes both the appropriation of land and the accumulation of stock, the whole produce of labour belongs to the labourer. He has neither landlord nor master to share with him.[1]

But then private property intervened, and since then workers have been forced to give part of their product to landlords and capitalists, because they don't own the land or the capital that they work with:

> But this original state of things, in which the labourer enjoyed the whole produce of his own labour, could not last beyond the first introduction of the appropriation of land and the accumulation of stock. . . . As soon as

land becomes private property, the landlord demands a share of almost all the produce which the labourer can either raise or collect from it. . . . The produce of almost all other labour is liable to the like deduction of profit.

Thus, according to Smith, profits are nothing but a deduction from the fruits of labor. But didn't he see that capitalists introduce improvements in production methods? Surely these entitle them to profits? According to Smith, had workers owned the total product that they produced, they would have used part of this product to introduce the improvements in productivity themselves:

> Had this state [workers owning the product they produce] continued, the wages of labour would have augmented with all those improvements in its productive powers, to which the division of labour gives occasion. All things would gradually have become cheaper. They would have been produced by a smaller quantity of labour.

The introduction of private property was not what spurred these improvements, according to Smith; private property came about long before any significant improvements were ever introduced:

> But this original state of things, in which the labourer enjoyed the whole produce of his own labour, could not last beyond the first introduction of the appropriation of land and the accumulation of stock. It was at an end, therefore, long before the most considerable improvements were made in the productive powers of labour.

If profits are just a deduction from the product that labor produces, what determines how large the deduction is? This, according to Smith, is determined by the bargaining power of the two parties. Usually the capitalist is the stronger party, because he has more holding power—an ability to bide his time before being paid:

The workmen desire to get as much, the masters to give as little, as possible. . . . It is not, however, difficult to foresee which of the two parties must, upon all ordinary occasions, have the advantage in the dispute, and force the other into a compliance with their terms. . . . In all such disputes, the masters can hold out much longer [because they are wealthier].

But even if capitalists generally have more bargaining power, that power is not always overwhelming. Smith pointed out that wages were different in different places, and that these differences were not due to differences in the cost of living:

The way in which the labouring poor buy all things, are generally fully as cheap, or cheaper, in great towns than in the remoter parts of the country. . . . But the wages of labour in a great town and its neighbourhood, are frequently a fourth or a fifth part, twenty or five-and-twenty per cent higher than at a few miles distance.

The reason that the employers do not always win to the same degree is that wealth is only one of the factors that determine bargaining power. The other factors include: (i) the ability of workers to form unions; (ii) the ability of employers to form their own unions, and, the most important factor of all, (iii) the ability of employers to use the power of the government to break the workers' unions:

[Workmen] are disposed to combine in order to raise, . . . [masters] in order to lower, the wages of labour. . . . The masters, upon these occasions [strikes and other labor actions] . . . never cease to call aloud for the assistance of the civil magistrate, and the rigorous execution of those laws which have been enacted with so much severity against the combination [union] of servants, labourers, and journeymen.

If workers succeed in getting higher wages, is this a good thing for the "wealth of nations"? According to Smith it is, because the well-being of workers is itself the "wealth of nations":

> Is this improvement in the circumstances of the lower ranks of the people to be regarded as an advantage or as an inconveniency to the society? The answer seems at first sight abundantly plain. Servants, labourers, and workmen of different kinds, make up the far greater part of every great political society. But what improves the circumstances of the greater part can never be regarded as an inconveniency to the whole. No society can surely be flourishing and happy, of which the far greater part of the members are poor and miserable. It is but equity, besides, that they who feed, cloath, and lodge the whole body of the people, should have such a share of the produce of their own labour as to be themselves tolerably well fed, cloathed, and lodged.

Don't high wages cause an increase in unemployment, as neo-classical economists argue? Smith did not consider this possibility. He did believe that there was a relationship between unemployment and wages, but he believed it ran in the opposite direction: high unemployment causes wages to fall and low unemployment causes wages to rise. What causes changes in the level of unemployment then? Not wages but events that occur outside the labor market: "It is because the demand for labour increases in years of sudden and extraordinary plenty, and diminishes in those of sudden and extraordinary scarcity, that the money price of labour sometimes rises in the one, and sinks in the other." What could such events be? Smith cited war as one possibility, but there are numerous other possibilities, not all man-made, such as weather that results in poor crops. Had he lived in our times Smith would no doubt have pointed to the loss in consumer and investor confidence following the subprime scandal as causes of the increase in unemployment rates.

FIGURE 9.1: ADAM SMITH, 1723–1790

"No society can surely be flourishing and happy, of which the far greater part of the members are poor and miserable."

Smith probably hoped that his book would convince the government to side with workers, but this did not happen. In 1800, ten years after his death, the British Parliament passed a Combination Act that decreed:

> Every . . . workman . . . who shall . . . enter into any combination to obtain an advance [increase] of wages, or to lessen or alter the hours or duration of the time of working, or to decrease the quantity of work, or for any other purpose . . . shall be committed to . . . gaol for any time not exceeding 3 calendar months; or otherwise be committed to some House of Correction . . . for any time not exceeding 2 calendar months.[2]

DAVID RICARDO (1772–1823)

The British economist David Ricardo continued Smith's work.[3] In 1815, English landowners prevailed on Parliament to pass a "Corn Law," which was a tariff on the imports of food. English industrialists opposed the tariff because they believed that higher food prices would lead to higher wages and thus lower profits. For Ricardo, a member of the London Stock Exchange, this situation presented an opportunity to investigate how prices are determined in general. Two theories resulted: one of wages and profits, and one of land rent.

Ricardo's theory of wages and profits was virtually the same as Adam Smith's. His theory of land rent broke new ground, however, because it introduced the concept of "diminishing marginal productivity." Ricardo believed that this concept applied only in agriculture, and that even there it did not apply to individual workers, but only to combinations of workers and the capital goods they work with. As we shall see in the next chapter, Clark would later apply the concept to individual workers and make it into his own theory of wages.

Ricardo's Theory of Wages and Profits

According to Ricardo a worker earns a wage that is equal to the value of the goods that she requires to subsist. He called this wage the "natural price" of labor. Ricardo emphasized, though, that the "natural price" of labor is *not* determined by nature but by "habit and custom": "It is not to be understood that the natural price of labour, estimated even in food and necessaries, is absolutely fixed and constant. It varies at different times in the same country, and very materially differs in different countries. It essentially depends on the habits and customs of the people."[4] But how are the "habit and custom" of a time and a country determined? And what makes the wage rise when the price of food rises, as it does when the government passes a "Corn Law"? Ricardo did not say, perhaps because he expected his readers to be familiar with Smith's explanation in *The Wealth of Nations* that workers and employers haggle over wages, and that the final result is determined by their relative power.

Profits are a residue, according to this explanation. A firm sells its product in a market in which there are many other firms that also sell exactly the same product; the firm cannot raise the price it charges above the price of its competitors, and the firm is therefore a "price taker." The firm sells its product for the "market price" and collects revenue. Out of this revenue the firm pays for the factors of production: raw materials, electricity, maintenance, wear and tear on capital goods (machines and buildings), and labor. The money left over is the firm's profit. Hence, assuming that the price that a firm can charge for a product is constant, a higher wage means a lower profit, and vice versa.

RICARDO'S THEORY OF LAND RENT

In Ricardo's model, agricultural production involves three parties: a landlord who owns a field, workers who sell their labor, and a farmer who rents the field from its landlord and hires workers to till the field with capital goods that the farmer owns (a horse and a plow are an example of capital goods). The farmer sells the food that is produced and uses the proceeds to pay rent to the landlord and wages to the workers. The level of the wage is determined by "habit and custom," with which we are already familiar. The level of the rent is determined by the fertility of the field, as will be explained below. The residue after the rent and the wages are paid is the profit of the farmer; it can be regarded as the payment for the capital goods that she equipped the workers with and for the farmer's organizational and managerial work.

Of course, farmers are free to enter or leave farming at will. If profits in farming are lower than profits in industry, farmers will become industrialists. This will increase the supply of industrial goods and cause prices of industrial goods, and therefore industrial profits, to decline, until the equality between the profits in industry and the profits in agriculture is restored. The law of one price that was already introduced in the first part of the book is thus paralleled by the law of one profit.

To simplify his theory, Ricardo made three assumptions. First, he assumed that each worker uses exactly the same set of tools or capital goods; the combination of a worker and the tools she works with makes a unit Ricardo called a "dose." Second, each field is tilled by exactly one dose. Third, the doses are interchangeable, with no difference in productivity between them.

Fields differ in their fertility, and the more fertile the field, the more productive the dose that tills it. Because of competition between farmers for fields, the rent for a field fully reflects its fertility. The exact rent on any given field is calculated by taking the rent on the least fertile field and adding to it the difference between the value of the crop of this field and the value of the crop of the least fertile field.

Table 9.1 contains Ricardo's own figures and can be used to explore the relationship between the payment to a dose (which consists of the worker's wage plus the farmer's profit), the number of fields brought into production, and the rent on each field.[5] The second column lists the product of each field (bushels of wheat) when it is tilled. Ricardo called this the "marginal product of a dose," because it shows by how much the total product increases when that field is added to production. The marginal product of the first dose increases the total by 180 bushels, the second by 170, and so on, reflecting the decreasing fertility of the land. Ricardo could have called it the "marginal product of a dose and a field," but he left the field out because the field is always there, even when it is not being tilled. The last column of the table, the "Value of Marginal Product," or VMP, is simply the second column multiplied by the price of a bushel, under the assumption that the price of a bushel is 50¢.

TABLE 9.1: WHEAT PRODUCTION

DOSES OF INPUT/ FIELD NUMBER	MARGINAL PRODUCT OF DOSE (BUSHELS)	TOTAL OUTPUT (BUSHELS)	VALUE OF MARGINAL PRODUCT (1 BUSHEL = 50¢)
1	180	180	$90
2	170	350	$85
3	160	510	$80
4	150	660	$75

What is the rent on each field? This is determined by subtracting the remuneration of a dose (the sum of the wage of the worker and the profit that the farmer collects) from the income produced. Suppose that prevailing remuneration of a dose is $82.50. The farmer who rents the most fertile field sells $90 worth of food; after paying the dose (i.e., paying the worker and herself) she has $7.50 left for rent. (She may wish that she could keep this sum to herself, but she is in competition with other farmers for fields, and this assures that the rent she pays is $7.50.) The same calculation is repeated for the second field. The farmer who rents that slightly less fertile field sells $85 worth of food. He must still pay the dose $82.50, so he pays the difference—$2.50—in rent. But no farmer would rent the third field, because the value of the crop from that field is $80, less than the remuneration of the dose. The VMP schedule of the different fields is depicted in figure 9.2.

What would happen if the remuneration of a dose rose above $85? In this case one dose would become unemployed. If, however, the remuneration of a dose declined below $80, one additional dose would be hired.

It is important to note that given the remuneration of doses, the number of fields in production adjusts itself so that that remuneration is

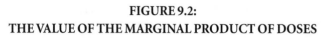

FIGURE 9.2:
THE VALUE OF THE MARGINAL PRODUCT OF DOSES

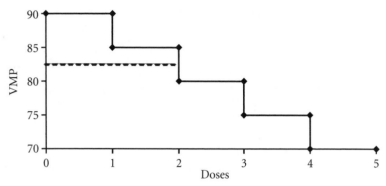

roughly equal to the VMP of the dose that tills the least fertile field in production. In our example the remuneration is $82.50 and the VMP of the dose that tills the least fertile field is $85. If the remuneration were only $72.50, two more fields would have been added to production, and the value of marginal product of the dose that tills the least fertile field would have been $75. In fact there are many fields, and the change in fertility from one field to the next is probably small. This means that in reality the line in figure 9.2 is smooth instead of stepwise, and that the remuneration of a dose is either very close, or actually equal to, the VMP of the dose tilling the least fertile land.

VMP IN INDUSTRY

Production in industry is often carried out not by workers and capital goods doses, but by teams made of a large number of workers who per-

FIGURE 9.3: DAVID RICARDO, 1772–1823

"[T]he natural price of labour . . . essentially depends on the habits and customs of the people."

Credit: W. Hall; photo courtesy the Library of Congress

form different tasks with different machines and with different skills. What does not play a role in industrial production, however, is the fertility of the land. Therefore, unlike the VMP of doses in agriculture, according to Ricardo the VMP curve of teams in industry is flat, as shown in figure 9-4.[6] While in agriculture doubling the number of doses may require tilling less fertile land, in industry doubling the number of teams means doubling production.

THE VMP OF INDIVIDUAL WORKERS

In agriculture the remuneration of a dose equals the VMP of the dose that tills the least fertile land, or the "marginal dose." In industry, the VMP of all teams is the same, and the remuneration of any team is, therefore, equal to its own VMP. Does a similar relationship exist also between

FIGURE 9.4: THE VALUE OF THE MARGINAL PRODUCT OF TEAMS IN INDUSTRY

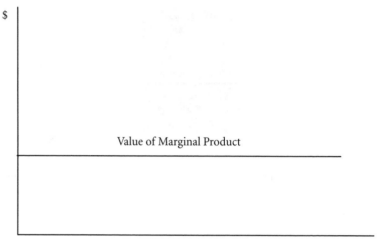

wages or profits and VMPs? Is a worker's wage equal to the VMP of workers, and are the profits of the owners of capital goods equal to the VMP of these goods?

According to Ricardo the division of the product of the dose between the worker and the farmer (who owns the capital goods that the worker uses) is determined by "habit and custom." Why not by VMPs? Because the product of a worker without capital goods (horse and plow) is zero, and so is the product of capital goods without the worker. Or, instead of interpreting the marginal products as zeros, it is possible to regard them as inseparable from the productivity of the dose to which they belong, and therefore immeasurable.

The use of capital goods is, of course, not limited to agriculture. We have already observed that a driver without a taxi cannot provide a trip and neither can a taxi without a driver, and that means that the VMP of each is zero or immeasurable.

It is often the case that the marginal product of any worker or machine, or even of any group of workers together with their machines, is not measurable, unless all the workers and all the machines are grouped together. Thus, all the workers and all the machines that are involved in the construction of a building—be they the operators of the earth-moving machines and the machines that they operate, the laborers who pour concrete and the concrete pumps that they use, the metal workers who erect the frame and the cranes that lift the metal to them, the plumbers with their tools and the electricians with theirs—together form just one team. The marginal product of the team is a high-rise. But the marginal product of each of these workers or each of the machines they operate is not measurable. A Russian folktale teaches this lesson best.

THE GIANT TURNIP

There once was a farmer who wanted to eat a turnip, so he went to his field to pull it out of the ground. He pulled and he pulled, but no matter how hard he pulled, the turnip did not come out of the ground. The farmer called to his wife for help. "My wife, my wife," he called, "please help me. I pulled and I pulled, but the turnip will not come out of the ground." So the wife pulled the husband who pulled the turnip, but the turnip did not come out of the ground. The farmer and his wife then asked their son for help and, when this did not make a difference, they also asked their daughter; they kept adding more and more members to their team until all the humans and all the animals on the farm were pulling. The cat pulled the dog that pulled the pig that pulled the bull that pulled the cow that pulled the daughter who pulled the son who

FIGURE 9.5: TEAM PRODUCTION

Credit: Illustration by Len Munnik in *The Tale of the Turnip* by Jim Forest, first published in 1988 by Marshall Pickering, Basingstoke, England

pulled the wife who pulled the farmer who pulled the turnip, but the turnip still did not budge. When there was nobody else to call, they called the last animal on the farm, the tiny mouse. "Little mouse, little mouse," they called, "please help us. We pulled and pulled, but the turnip would not come out." And it was only when the mouse added her effort that the turnip did come out.

What was the marginal product of the mouse? The whole turnip, because without her there would have been no turnip. And what was the marginal product of any other member of the team? The same whole turnip, because without any one of them there would have been no turnip. (The marginal product of each member of the team is also zero, because without all the rest of the members of the team the turnip would have stayed in the ground.) Yet the different members of the team could not each get paid the value of her marginal product because there was only one turnip to be had. Obviously, the process of production could not tell us how the turnip would or should be divided among its producers. Of course, they could all agree to divide it equally, but a true-to-life ending would have had somebody earning "the lion's share," in line with Smith's and Ricardo's theory of wages.

10.

THE NEO-CLASSICAL THEORY OF WAGES: JOHN BATES CLARK

For most of the nineteenth century, the working day went from sunrise to sunset, and the pay was not per hour but for per day. In 1884, American workers launched a campaign to limit the working day to eight hours, and they set a target date for achieving this goal: May 1, 1886. When that date arrived without any limits on the working day, workers demonstrated in cities all around the country, including Chicago. These demonstrations were all peaceful, but two days later, on May 3, the Chicago police attacked unarmed striking workers of the McCormick Reaper Company, killing six. A protest rally took place the following day in the city's Haymarket Square, and the police attacked this rally as well. A bomb exploded among the attacking police and one police officer was killed; the police then fired shots randomly into the crowd. The total number of dead and injured is not known because families were afraid to report their losses. Several cops were also injured, mostly from bullets fired by other officers.[1] Following the Haymarket Massacre eight labor leaders were convicted of murder because they had engaged in "inflammatory speeches and publications," and sentenced to death; four were hanged.[2]

Given this social unrest, John Bates Clark, a professor of economics at Columbia University, framed the questions facing economists:

The welfare of the laboring classes depends on whether they get much or little; but their attitude toward other classes—and, therefore, the stability of the social state—depends chiefly on the question, whether the amount that they get, be it large or small, is what they produce. If they create a small amount of wealth and get the whole of it, they may not seek to revolutionize society; but if it were to appear that they produce an ample amount and get only a part of it, many of them would become revolutionists, and all would have the right to do so. The indictment that hangs over society is that of "exploiting labor." "Workmen" it is said, "are regularly robbed of what they produce. This is done within the forms of law, and by the natural working of competition." If this charge were proved, every right-minded man should become a socialist; and his zeal in transforming the industrial system would then measure and express his sense of justice. If we are to test the charge, however, we must enter the realm of production. We must resolve the product of social industry into its component elements, in order to see whether the natural effect of competition is or is not to give to each producer the amount of wealth that he specifically brings into existence.[3]

Clark took this task upon himself. In 1899 he published a new theory of wages—a marginal productivity theory—that argued that "the natural effect of competition is . . . to give to each producer the amount of wealth that he specifically brings into existence." (At the same time in Europe another economist, Pareto, was busy battling Utilitarianism and calls for income redistribution.) Clark's theory consists of the assertion that workers earn the value of their marginal product.

CLARK'S THEORY OF WAGES

Ricardo made it clear that his analysis of the VMP of doses cannot be applied to the wages of the worker versus the profit of the owner of the capital goods that the worker uses, because the product of one member of the team is not separable from the product of all the others. Clark simply ignored this. His great contribution to economics is the claim that wages are determined by the VMP of workers, which Clark (unlike Ricardo) felt *could* be quantified. To convince his readers, he used the example of a steamship and applied it to all other industries:

> Though a hundred men can sail a steamship, a hundred and five may sail it better. . . . If new men are thus taken, their whole product is given to them. . . . in mills, mines, shops, furnaces, etc., there is in this way often a chance to vary, within narrow limits, the number of men who are employed, without affecting the owners' incomes. If new men are thus taken, their whole product is given to them.[4]

The condition "without affecting the owner's income" means that the workers are added to production without the addition of capital goods; this is necessary because otherwise it would be impossible to separate the marginal productivity of the additional worker from the productivity of that worker together with the capital goods she would be working with (capital goods are owned by the employer). Alas, Clark's own example serves to highlight how impossible this condition is. If more sailors are added to the ship, extra fuel and food will have to be added too, and sleeping and living accommodations will have to be created for them as well. And with the steam engines burning more coal, the kitchen processing more food, and the plumbing handling more refuse, it may even be necessary to add sailors to adapt the crew to its larger size. Thus, both because employing sailors on a ship requires a capital investment, and because sailing a ship is team (crew) production, Clark's method of measuring an individual sailor's marginal product is impossible. Beyond that, how would an additional captain or an additional cook make a ship "sail better"?

Neither Clark nor any other economist since has come up with a method for measuring the marginal product of labor because it is challenging to find a production process in which it would be possible to add a worker without adding any capital, and because it is impossible to isolate a given worker's VMP. What would an extra operator of the asphalt-grinding machine in the photograph that follows, or an extra dump truck driver, do without an extra machine or truck? And what would an extra supervisor do without an extra crew to supervise? Not only are the marginal productivities of the individual members of the asphalt grinding team zero, but the marginal productivity of the whole asphalt-grinding team is zero as well, because unless new asphalt is laid, there is no road. While the asphalt-grinding team is productive, the productivity of each of its members, whether worker or machine, is not separable from that of the rest, and it therefore cannot be quantified.

Yet, without even one example in which the marginal product of labor in any firm has actually been measured, Clark and neo-classical economists depict a VMP of labor curve that is a copy of Ricardo's curve of the marginal product of doses in agriculture. Ricardo believed that his marginal productivity theory applied only to doses, not to labor, and he also claimed that the decrease in marginal productivity of doses occurs in agriculture but not in industry. The neo-classical economists remove all of Ricardo's qualifications, claiming that the marginal productivity of a worker is separable from the productivity of the team that she belongs to, that workers can be added to production without any addition of tools or capital goods, and that as workers are added to production in this way

FIGURE 10.1: ASPHALT GRINDING

their marginal product diminishes. All three claims are made not for special cases, but as a general rule.

Figure 10.2 presents Clark's neo-classical theory of wages. In the production of any good there is a VMP of workers' curve and it is downward sloping, mimicking Ricardo's VMP curve for doses in agriculture. When the wage is W_0, L_0 workers are hired. But when the wage increases to W_1, only L_1 are hired, because the marginal product of workers diminishes. In either case, the last worker hired is paid the value of her marginal product, or full value of the product she has produced. And since the workers are interchangeable, any worker could have been the last worker hired, and any worker is therefore paid the full value of the product she has produced.

With the conjuring of a separable and quantifiable marginal product

FIGURE 10.2:
NEO-CLASSICAL VALUE OF MARGINAL PRODUCT

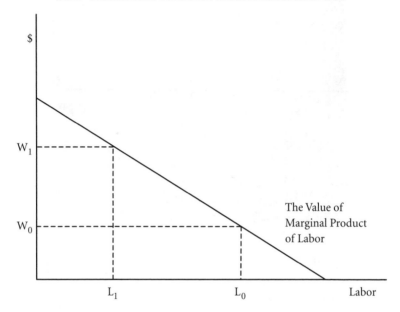

of labor that is diminishing for each additional worker added, Clark's mission was accomplished. We now "see" that "the natural effect of competition is . . . to give to each producer the amount of wealth that he specifically brings into existence." If workers' demand for higher wages were met, the result would be unemployment. The only problem with this argument is, of course, that the VMP of labor simply does not exist. The VMP curve in figure 10.2 is fiction, because the VMP of labor is not separable from the product of the team that she is a member of, and workers cannot be added into production one by one, without any additions of capital goods or other workers.

How do economists convince their students that the marginal product of labor is separable and diminishing with each added worker? What evidence do they cite? Because there is no evidence, each economics professor is left to invent his own parable. According to the author of the Wikipedia entry on labor economics:

> An example is the employment of labour in the use of trucks to transport goods. Assuming the number of available trucks (capital) is fixed, then the amount of the variable input labour could be varied and the resultant efficiency determined. At least one labourer (the driver) is necessary. Additional workers per vehicle could be productive in loading, unloading, navigation, or around the clock continuous driving. But at some point the returns to investment in labour will start to diminish and efficiency will decrease. The most efficient distribution of labour per piece of equipment will likely be one driver plus an additional worker for other tasks (2 workers per truck would be more efficient than 5 per truck).[5]

And according to Barnes & Noble's *Spark Notes:*

> Imagine, for instance, that a small furniture store is hiring workers. One worker will get a good deal done on his own. The second worker will probably be productive, as well. The sixteenth worker, however, would probably get nothing done, since there wouldn't be enough space or tools to make furniture. Between the second and the sixteenth worker, we would see a gradual drop in marginal productivity, a trend we call the Law of Diminishing Returns: additional workers may add to productivity, but each worker contributes less, until the marginal product (MP) is 0.[6]

In the popular textbook *Intermediate Economics* by Hal Varian, mentioned above in our discussion of Pareto efficiency, the author assures readers that there is a "law of diminishing marginal product [of any factor of production]. It isn't really a 'law,' " Varian writes, "it's just a common feature of most kinds of production processes." [7] And since this is a "feature of most production processes," the value of the marginal product of labor is the only theory of wages that Varian presents.

The problem with these statements is that, despite their implicit claim that they are derived from everyday experience, everyday experience actually contradicts them. First, the examples themselves do not show what their authors say they show. Dump trucks that move earth to and from construction sites travel short distances and have no use for either additional drivers or for workers to unload them. The same is true for cement trucks, since they unload their cargo automatically into concrete pumps. The marginal productivity of a second driver in all these cases would be zero, but so is the marginal product of the actual driver, because without a truck, she would not have been able to deliver anything at all. How then can trucks be an example for diminishing marginal productivity of workers and for how the VMP of workers explains workers' wages?

As for the *Spark Notes* claim—that if the marginal productivity of the second carpenter in a furniture factory is high and of the sixteenth carpenter is zero, then the marginal productivity of the carpenters in between must be declining gradually—this is doubtful. As the photograph below shows, carpenters work on benches and with tools, and Ricardo's dose is perhaps the best description for such a method of production. Except for differences due to individual dexterity, the marginal product of all doses is exactly the same, while the marginal product of a carpenter without a bench and tools is zero.

Even more troubling, however, is the fact that students' attention is diverted from the ubiquitous examples that are blatantly inconsistent with the VMP theory of wages. Why is it that trucks are discussed, but not taxis and buses? Is it because in these cases it is so obvious that the marginal productivities of the drivers are not separable from the capital goods they drive? Why is a parable drawn from a furniture factory when

FIGURE 10.3: FURNITURE FACTORY

Source: Photo Library, The Burrell Collection, Glasgow

very few students have ever seen one, yet students' attention is not called to team production, even though every construction site or road that is being paved displays it so clearly? How can Varian assure his readers that declining marginal productivity is a "feature of most production processes," when most production processes that students witness every day contradict this claim?

Had students known of Clark's fear of social unrest by workers who felt exploited and of the historical events that gave rise to his fear, their antennae might have been raised. Without such discussion, they accept the diminishing VMP of labor he conjured as a scientific observation, and pass this fabrication on to their own students. And among economists, Clark is revered: each year the American Economic Association awards the John Bates Clark Medal to the economist who has made the most important contributions to the field before the age of forty.

FIGURE 10.4: JOHN BATES CLARK, 1847–1938

"The indictment that hangs over society is that of 'exploiting labor.' . . . If this charge were proved, every right-minded man should become a socialist. . . ."

Source: Photo courtesy John Bates Clark Papers, Rare Book and Manuscript Library, Columbia University

11

THE EVIDENCE

At the beginning of the twentieth century the classical theory of wages (based on the observation that workers' marginal productivities are not separable) was replaced by the neo-classical theory (which states that they are). Does any empirical evidence justify this switch? Has the marginal productivity of an individual worker ever been measured separately from the productivity of the team that she works with? No and no. In one way this is not surprising. The evidence that the VMP theory of wages is wrong is all around us and in plain sight. How can the VMP theory explain the wage of a bus driver when the productivity of a driver cannot be separated from the productivity of driver and bus? And what's true for a bus driver and her bus is equally true for CEOs, who exploit to great advantage the fact that individual contributions cannot be measured in team production. Hank McKinnell became the CEO of Pfizer in 2001, and during the five years that he was on the job, the value of Pfizer's share declined by 46 percent (figure 11.1). Yet McKinnell received $65 million in compensation during this period. During the Q&A period at a shareholders' meeting, Rajesh Kumar, an orthopedic surgeon and a Pfizer shareholder, asked why Mr. McKinnell, with his record, received in two days what he as a surgeon earned over the course of one year. McKinnell was neither required to respond to the question, nor return any of the money. On the contrary, while shareholders' anger caused him to retire, he received a retirement package that included an additional $180 million. Because marginal products are not separable, no one, including the board, could show that the decline was his marginal product, or that he personally had not produced $65 million worth of product. Dana G. Mead, the chair of Pfizer's compensation committee (as well as the chair of the board of trustees of MIT), explained that McKinnell's pay was based on "market forces" and that was that.[1]

The lengthy strike in 2007–8 by television writers in the United States was a transparent demonstration that what determines how the product of a team is divided between its members is not what each member has produced, but rather naked force. Viewers may regard the writer as the

FIGURE 11.1: PFIZER UNDER MCKINNELL

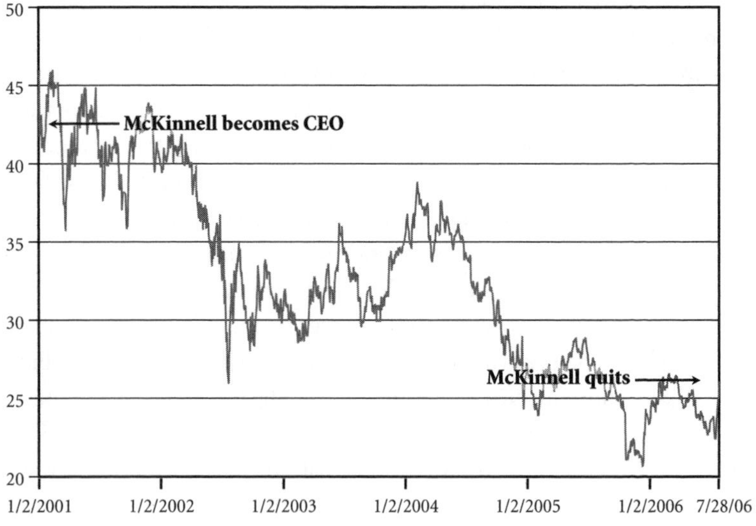

Source: Based on a chart at: http://iproceed.com/images/pfizer-stock-chart.jpg

most crucial person in the success of a show, but in reality what determines the writers' pay is not their central role but their ability to unite and fight together with other writers against their employers (who claim that it is their money that makes the show possible to begin with).

No empirical tests are needed to verify that in the vast majority of cases the marginal product of each individual worker or each unit of capital is not separable from the product of the team that she is part of, and it is therefore interesting that economists have so successfully been able to ignore this fundamental flaw in neo-classical wage theory. In 1984, however, eighty-five years after Clark conjured the marginal productivity theory of wages, the economist Robert Frank searched for and found one profession in which, he believed, the marginal productivity of an individual worker is separable: sales. He investigated whether in this one profession workers earn the value of their marginal product, and claimed to have discovered that they don't. But as we shall see, since it is unclear whether the marginal productivity of a salesperson is in fact separable or whether the salesperson and the firm she works for constitute a team, Frank's evidence is probably not valid.

In 2001 the economists Orley Ashenfelter and Štěpán Jurajda took another approach to testing the VMP theory of wages. If workers' marginal products are separable and measureable, then two workers who produce exactly the same product with exactly the same tools and exactly the same inputs should earn exactly the same wage. Yet, as we shall see, Ashenfelter and Jurajda discovered that the disparity in wages among workers, who, according to the theory, have identical marginal productivities, is enormous.

SALESPEOPLE

At first blush it may appear that measuring the marginal productivity of salespeople would be entirely simple. Robert Frank believed so, and this is what he attempted to do in his study "Are Workers Paid Their Marginal Product?" [2]

In many parts of the country a sale of a home involves two stages. In the first, a "listing agent" finds a seller and lists the home for sale in a "multiple listing." That listing is open to all real estate agents. In the second stage any real estate agent, of any firm, may find a buyer for that home. The firm that employs the "listing agent" is known as the "listing firm," and it normally receives 40 percent of the commission that the seller pays. The firm that employs the "selling agent" is the "selling firm," and it receives 60 percent of the commission. Each of these firms then divides its share of its commission between the firm itself and its respective agent.

Frank is aware that the marginal productivity of the listing agent cannot be separated from the marginal productivity of the listing firm, because while it is the agent who obtains the listing, it is the firm that advertises the sale. But Frank argues that when a selling agent finds a buyer for the home, this is due strictly to her own effort, and that the firm she works for contributes nothing to the selling agent's success. Therefore, if the selling agency receives a $5,000 commission, all of it is the marginal product of the selling agent, and if she were paid the value of her marginal product, the full sum would have been passed on to her. (The selling agent has a desk and phone in the firm's office, but the charge for these should be a flat fee.) Yet Frank discovered that depending on whom she works for, the selling agent normally gets only between 50 percent and 57.5 percent of the $5,000. Therefore, Frank concluded, selling agents do not earn the value of their marginal product.

In a similar vein Frank discovered that the pay of car salespeople diverges even further from their VMP. In a typical firm, a salesperson receives a base pay and about 25 percent of the additional profits that she generates for the car dealership. The base pay structure is fundamentally inconsistent with the VMP theory of wages. Therefore, car salespeople are also not paid the value of their marginal product, Frank concluded.

But despite Frank's assurances, it is not clear that in the cases he cites firms have nothing to contribute. If a selling firm has nothing to contribute, why would the selling agent join it to begin with? And why would a car salesperson not work from her own home if she can sell cars without any boost from her dealer's lot?

What the firms may contribute in both cases is reliability. Suppose that the selling agent misrepresented the condition of the house she was selling. Who would the buyer complain to if the agent had left town or did not have sufficient assets with which to pay compensation? In the case of a car salesperson, reliability may play an even bigger role, because if the car is broken, the buyer can return it to the dealer for repair. If there were no dealer, however, whom would the buyer return to?

There are cases in which workers do work with only their bare hands, with no capital and no direct collaboration with other workers. Picking fruit is such a case. But even in this case, the worker is part of a team, because before the fruit could be picked, the tree had to be planted, watered, and sprayed, and after it was picked the fruit had to be shipped to market and then sold. The product of a single fruit picker is not separable from the product of the team.

What the case of fruit pickers shows clearly is how government policy and its enforcement determine the strength of workers relative to the strength of employers, and ultimately the share that each party receives of the product that the two parties produced together. Immigration determines how many workers compete for fruit-picking jobs. With a lax enforcement of immigration laws the supply of workers is practically endless, and as a result wages in agriculture are so low that Americans do not want to do these jobs.

BIG MAC WAGES

If workers earn the value of their marginal product, then two workers who have the same marginal product should receive the same pay. The economists Orley Ashenfelter and Štěpán Jurajda tested whether this was the case as part of a study that compared wages around the globe.[3] To discover whether wages in one country are higher than wages in another, Ashenfelter and Jurajda needed to compare wages for a job that is identical across borders. Entry-level jobs at McDonald's meet this criterion, because they are identical no matter where they are performed. But while the jobs are the same, the currencies are not. How can a wage in one currency be compared with the wage in another? Instead of measuring wages in currencies, Ashenfelter and Jurajda measured wages in Big Macs. Suppose that the marginal product of a McDonald's worker is two Big Macs per hour. If the VMP theory of wages is correct, then each McDonald's worker around the globe should be paid the value of two Big Macs per hour, no matter what currency is involved. The money value of two Big Macs is immaterial. What matters is whether in Big Macs per hour the wage across countries is the same. Table 11.1 shows Ashenfelter and Jurajda's findings.

TABLE 11.1: BIG MAC WAGES AROUND THE WORLD

COUNTRY	CASHIER AND CREW, AUGUST 2000 BIG MAC PER HOUR OF WORK
India	0.23
Columbia	0.23
China	0.36
Indonesia	0.36
Venezuela	0.41
Thailand	0.43
Philippines	0.46
Russia	0.47
Brazil	0.54
Argentina	0.60
Malaysia	0.70
Korea	0.70
Turkey	0.75
Czech Republic	0.82
Poland	0.86
Taiwan	0.94
Singapore	1.25
Hong Kong	1.42
Italy (2001)	2.04
UK	2.11
Germany	2.25
Canada	2.40
USA	2.59
Sweden	2.60
Belgium	2.65
France	2.72
Japan	3.04

As the table shows, McDonald's workers, who produce the same marginal products, earn very different amounts, depending on where they live. A Chinese worker doing exactly the same job as an American worker earns one-seventh of the Big Macs that an American worker earns.

Ashenfelter and Jurajda then converted the wages of workers in manufacturing and construction into dollars, and they discovered that the ratios between the wages of workers across countries in construction are the same as they are for McDonald's workers. What can explain these differences? Ashenfelter and Jurajda attribute the differences to organizational and structural differences, but they don't spell these out. Competition from workers who move to cities from the countryside in the developing world, and the absence of a minimum wage law in these countries, are perhaps the main reasons that wages in these countries are lower. Adam Smith would have pointed out that a glut of labor weakens workers' negotiating power vis-à-vis their employers, and it is also possible that workers' poverty reduces their ability to force their government to pass minimum wage laws. It is clear that the VMP theory of wages is inconsistent with the data while the classical theory of wages is supported by the data.

12

THE MINIMUM WAGE

According to the VMP theory of wages, a minimum wage that is above the wage determined by the market would cause firms to fire workers. This is shown using a typical declining VMP of labor curve in figure 12.1. When the wage is determined by the free market it is W_c (c stands for competitive), and at this wage L_c workers are employed. If the wage is raised by law to W_{min} (min stands for minimum), all of a sudden the values of the marginal products of all the workers beyond L_{min} are below the wage that the employers must pay, and the workers in the interval $L_{min}-L_c$ become unemployed.

EMPLOYERS' RESPONSE TO MINIMUM WAGE: THE EVIDENCE

Do employers hire fewer workers when the minimum wage is increased? The question was investigated by the economists David Card and Alan Krueger.[1] On April 1, 1992, the minimum wage in the state of New Jersey increased from $4.25, the federal minimum, to $5.05. Card and Krueger contacted Burger King, KFC, Wendy's, and Roy Rogers outlets one month before and eight months after that date and asked them how many employees they had each time. Card and Krueger note that chains

FIGURE 12.1: THE MINIMUM WAGE REDUCES EMPLOYMENT

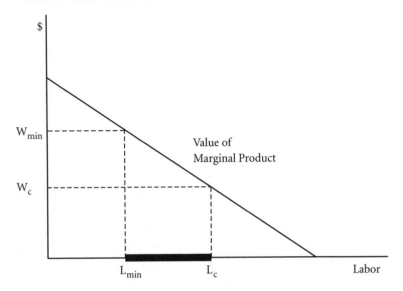

provide the best indicator of employers' response to a change in the minimum wage because they are more likely to comply with the minimum wage laws than are independent stores.[2]

Since the minimum wage was not the only economic change to occur over the nine-month period, Card and Krueger used a control group—the outlets of the same chains in neighboring eastern Pennsylvania—to isolate the effect of the change in the minimum wage in New Jersey from the effect of other changes. Pennsylvania's minimum wage stayed at $4.25 during the same period. Table 12.1 summarizes Card and Krueger's findings.

TABLE 12.1: EMPLOYMENT BEFORE AND
AFTER INCREASE OF MINIMUM WAGE

	NJ	PA
One Month Before Increase		
Full-Time Equivalent Employment	20.40	23.30
Percentage Full-Time Employees	32.80	35.00
Wage = $4.25 (%)	30.50	32.90
Price of Full Meal	$3.35	$3.04
Hours Open (Weekdays)	14.40	14.50
Eight Months After Increase		
FTE Employment	21.00	21.20
Percentage Full-Time Employees	35.90	30.40
Wage = $4.25 (%)	0.00	25.30
Wage = $5.05 (%)	85.20	1.30
Price of full meal	$3.41	$3.03
Hours Open (Weekdays)	14.40	14.70

The table shows that following the increase in the minimum wage, employment virtually did not change in New Jersey while in Pennsylvania employment decreased. A store in New Jersey employed on average slightly more than twenty workers before the change, and twenty-one workers after. A store in Pennsylvania employed twenty-three workers before and twenty-one workers after. Thus a significant increase in the minimum wage does not necessarily cause the level of employment to decrease.

Table 12.1 also shows that the increase in the minimum wage benefited a large number of employees. Before the increase, 31 percent of employees in these chains in New Jersey earned the minimum wage of $4.25. After the increase, 85 percent of employees earned the new minimum wage of $5.05. This indicates that, before the increase, there were many workers who earned *more* than the *old* minimum wage but were at or *below* the *new* minimum wage.

It is sometimes asserted that when the minimum wage increases, employers find other ways of decreasing workers' pay. Fast food chains provide their employees free or reduced price meals, for instance, but Card and Krueger discovered that there was no change in these policies after the increase in the minimum wage.

When the chains had to pay their workers more, they also charged their customers more: the prices of meals in New Jersey increased by about 2 percent after the increase in the minimum wage. This creates a new puzzle. With the higher prices of meals, the number of meals that the restaurants sold has probably decreased. Why did the New Jersey restaurants not fire workers when their volume of business decreased? Some economists argue that higher wages increase labor productivity by decreasing absenteeism and turnover, and improving workers' morale. But the increase in the minimum wage was 19 percent, and it's hard to imagine that such changes in workers' behavior could increase productivity by even a small fraction of this number. Moreover, even if the increase in prices did not cause sales to fall, surely sales did not increase. With the same level of sales an increase in productivity would have resulted in more workers being fired, not fewer. But as we show below, the puzzle of why workers were not fired is not a puzzle at all, once we realize that production is done by teams.

TEAM PRODUCTION AND THE MINIMUM WAGE

As table 12.1 shows, a restaurant in the Card and Krueger study employed twenty people over two shifts, or ten workers per shift. It is tempting to conclude that if one worker in each shift is let go, production will decline by about 10 percent, but this is actually not the case. The *function* of each employee must be taken into account. For instance, when a store with ten workers and three cash registers employs one fewer cashier, the store's capacity to handle customers is diminished by 33 percent, not 10 percent. In the rear of fast food restaurants, production is organized along an assembly line involving fewer than ten workers. Removing one worker from this line would slow production by more than 10 percent also. This is why even a 19 percent increase in the minimum wage did not result in the firing of workers.[3] Because of the increase in the minimum wage, workers earn a little bit more, customers pay a little bit more, and employers probably earn a little bit less. Little else changes.

Of course, there are limits to how high wages can rise without affecting employment. Employers must earn a profit to stay in business. The demand for labor that the workers in New Jersey's fast food industry faced is depicted in figure 12.2. If the wage is below W_{max}, employers will need L_0 workers. Bargaining between employers and workers will determine where in the range from zero to W_{max} the wage will fall, and therefore also what the level of profits will be. The New Jersey law set the minimum wage at a level below W_{max} (and above zero profits), simultaneously improving the lives of burger flippers and, in the state whose slogan is "Come See for Yourself," disproving the neo-classical theory that any increase in wages will result in lost jobs.

FIGURE 12.2: THE DEMAND FOR LABOR WITH TEAM PRODUCTION

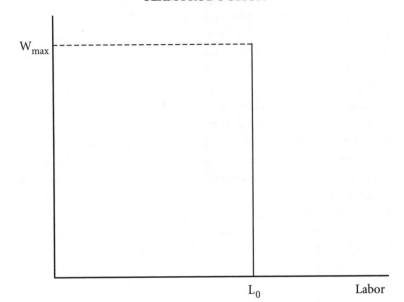

13

THEORIES OF WAGES AND THE GREAT DEPRESSION

In the years 1929–39 the United States, along with the rest of the world, experienced an economic downturn so deep and so long that it was called the Great Depression. The meaning of the Great Depression can best be summarized by a single statistic: the rate of unemployment. As table 13.1 shows, in the middle of the Depression 25 percent of Americans were unemployed. Ten years after the start of the Depression, the rate of unemployment was still 17.2 percent.

What caused the Great Depression? The stakes in the answer are high, and it is not surprising that seventy years later there is still disagreement among economists about it. As we shall see, differing theories of wages are the source of much of the disagreement, and therefore these theories have tremendous relevance today.

TABLE 13.1: UNEMPLOYMENT, 1923–1942

YEAR	RATE
1923–29	3.3
1930	8.9
1931	15.9
1932	23.6

(continued)

TABLE 13.1: UNEMPLOYMENT, 1923–1942 *(continued)*

YEAR	RATE
1933	24.9
1934	21.7
1935	20.1
1936	17.0
1937	14.3
1938	19.0
1939	17.2
1940	14.6
1941	9.9
1942	4.7

Source: Robert Van Giezen and Albert E. Schwenk. "Compensation from before World War I through the Great Depression," Bureau of Labor Statistics, U.S. Department of Labor, 2003: http://www.bls.gov/opub/cwc/cm20030124ar03p1.htm

WAGES AND THE "PUZZLE" OF
THE GREAT DEPRESSION

In 1929, economists believed that the economy was self-regulating and that the crash would be followed by a short adjustment period that would return it to full employment. The adjustment process promised by economists should have started in the labor market and been simple. As we have seen, economists believe that the demand for labor is a VMP curve that, because of the "law of diminishing marginal product," is downward sloping. Therefore the lower the wage, the greater the number of workers that employers will want to hire. All that should have been required for unemployment to end was for wages to decline. But this adjustment did not happen. In fact, unemployment did not fall below 14 percent until World War II. Thus the Great Depression showed that a market economy is *not* self-regulating. It does not have a mechanism that always pulls it out of a recession, leaving us with the question, what is wrong with the view that falling wages will restore the economy to full employment?

One view, which the economist John Maynard Keynes (1883–1946) characterized as the "classical view," is that lower wages *would* have restored full employment, except that wages were "sticky": in spite of the high rate of unemployment workers refused to agree to decreases in their wages.[1] But to Keynes this view did not make sense:

> The contention that the unemployment which characterizes a depression is due to a refusal by labour to accept a reduction of money-wages is not clearly supported by the facts. It is not very plausible to assert that unemployment in the United States in 1932 was due either to labour obstinately refusing to accept a reduction of money-wages or to its obstinately demanding a real wage beyond what the productivity of the economic machine was capable of furnishing.[2]

Instead of blaming high wages for high unemployment, Keynes developed a new theory that—consistent with Adam Smith's view that the level of employment is not determined by wages—argues that falling wages can actually increase the level of unemployment instead of decreasing it.

KEYNES'S SOLUTION

According to Keynes, production takes place to satisfy two kinds of demand. One is a demand for consumer goods and the other is a demand for investment goods. The two together form the "aggregate demand." When the level of aggregate demand is high, the levels of production and employment are high. When the level of aggregate demand is low, so are the levels of production and employment.

The two demands that form the aggregate demand behave in very different ways. The demand by consumers for consumer goods follows a regular pattern: the higher people's income, the more they want to consume. The demand by investors for investment goods is far less regular, however, because this demand is determined by investors' level of optimism about the future. When investors are pessimistic, they curtail their demands, and the result is unemployment. The following example illustrates how the level of aggregate demand determines the level of production in the economy in Keynes's theory.

Suppose that when there is full employment, the economy produces a total of $100 worth of goods and services in a day. This $100 is also the sum total of the incomes and profits that the workers and employers who produce these goods and services earn. The households of the workers and employers use a fraction of their $100 income, say $90, to buy goods and services for consumption. (We assume that there are no imports or exports.) They save the remaining $10. If at the same time investors purchase $10 worth of investment goods, then production will continue at the same full employment level of $100 as before. Each period consumers and producers together will demand $100 worth of goods, these goods will be produced, and full employment will prevail. But if investors all of a sudden want to invest only $5, then $5 worth of goods and services would go unsold. In response, firms would cut their production level to $95, and momentarily this would also be the new level of income that the workers and their employers earn. But this would not be the end of the adjustment to the decline in investment. With an income of only $95, consumers would cut their consumption somewhat, and as a result employment and income would decline further. This secondary decline in income may itself lead to a tertiary decline in income. When will this downward spiral end? As long as consumers want to save a larger amount than investors want to invest, some goods go unsold, and employment and income decline. Stability, or equilibrium, is restored when the amount that investors want to invest matches the amount that consumers want to save. This can be illustrated by continuing our example.

Let's assume that consumers always save 10 percent and consume 90 percent of their income, regardless of what the level of their income is. Thus, when, due to the decrease in investment aggregate demand and income fall to $95, consumers reduce their consumption from $90 to $85.50. But this means that aggregate demand is now only $90.50 (because investment is $5), and this causes the level of production and income to decline to that level also (or goods will go unsold). With an income of $90.50 consumption is only $81, however, and aggregate demand is only $86; employment and income decline again. Eventually the level of income reaches a bottom of $50, though. With that level of income consumers want to consume $45, and since investors want to invest $5, aggregate demand is $50, exactly the same as income. All the goods produced are sold, and there is no buildup of unsold goods. Equilibrium is restored, but because production is at 50 percent of the full employment level, the unemployment rate is 50 percent.

Thus according to Keynes it is the level of investment, not the level of wages, that determines the level of unemployment. And rather than being self-correcting, the market system amplifies initial disturbances to it. A small decline in investment may lead to a manyfold-larger decrease in income and a correspondingly large increase in unemployment. Furthermore, Keynes argued, such declines are unavoidable.

According to Keynes, how much investors want to invest depends on their optimism about the future state of the economy. The task of the investor is to predict the future well-being of the economy, but that well-being depends on the level of optimism of all other investors. Thus each investor needs to know what predictions *other* investors are making about the predictions that *other* investors are making regarding the performance of the economy in the future. Of course, this type of analysis is simply not possible. Instead, investors must rely on "spontaneous optimism." As Keynes wrote:

> A large proportion of our positive activities depend on spontaneous optimism rather than on a mathematical expectation, whether moral or hedonistic or economic. Most, probably, of our decisions to do something positive, the full consequences of which will be drawn out over many days to come, can only be taken as a result of animal spirits—of a spontaneous urge to action rather than inaction, and not as the outcome of a weighted average of quantitative benefits multiplied by quantitative probabilities. Enterprise only pretends to itself to be mainly actuated by the statements in its own prospectus, however candid and sincere. Only a little more than an expedition to the South Pole, is it based on an exact calculation of benefits to come. Thus if the animal spirits are dimmed and the spontaneous optimism falters, leaving us to depend on nothing but a mathematical expectation, enterprise will fade and die;—though fears of loss may have a basis no more reasonable than hopes of profit had before.[3]

Because it is impossible to calculate what the "correct level of optimism" is, pessimism, once it sets in, can be long-lived. Keynes advocated, therefore, that when unemployment is high the government should step in, to increase the aggregate demand and boost production to the level of full employment.

Even if a decline in investment leads to an initial fall in employment and income, why wouldn't lower wages restore the economy to full employment, as the neo-classical economists argued? Because, Keynes explained, falling wages would lead to falling prices, and falling prices would make investments less worthwhile and investors more pessimistic. It is profitable to spend $5 today to sell a good for $6 tomorrow, but if tomorrow the good will sell for only $4, then the investor would

lose money. Therefore, instead of restoring the economy to full employment, falling wages only increase investors' pessimism, causing the aggregate demand to remain low.

ECONOMIC POLICIES DURING
THE GREAT DEPRESSION

What effect Keynes's theory had on President Franklin Delano Roosevelt
is not known. But FDR's policies were clearly designed to increase aggregate demand. First, his administration hired millions of workers directly.
In 1938, for example, the Works Progress Administration employed
three million workers in projects ranging from the creation of parks to
recording oral histories of former slaves. To remove some of investors'
fear of falling prices, the National Recovery Act of 1935 permitted producers to get together to fix prices, in clear violation of the antitrust acts
(as long as they agreed to pay above certain minimum wages that the
government dictated). And to encourage consumption, Congress moved
to strengthen the hand of workers when they negotiated wages with their
employers. The Wagner Act, also of 1935, decreed that once the majority
of workers voted for a union, all workers had to pay union dues.
Nonunion members could no longer free ride on the benefits that the
unions generated.

For economists and other stakeholders, however, Keynes's argument
that a free market system could not pull itself out of unemployment
without government intervention was problematic. The counterattack
started immediately following World War II.

FIGURE 13.1: JOHN MAYNARD KEYNES, 1883–1946

"It is not very plausible to assert that unemployment in the United States in 1932 was due either to labour obstinately refusing to accept a reduction of money-wages or to its obstinately demanding a real wage beyond what the productivity of the economic machine was capable of furnishing."

Source: Photo courtesy of the IMF

PIGOU AND PATINKIN: IF INVESTORS INVESTED LESS, CONSUMERS WOULD CONSUME MORE

World War II replaced the Depression-fighting hiring policies of the government with the recruitment of soldiers. The effect on unemployment was the same, but the demonstration that the government is the only economic actor that can reliably restore the level of employment was lost. It was, of course, the government that recruited the soldiers, but the purpose was to fight Germans, Italians, and Japanese, not unemployment, and the fact that full employment was restored through government hiring went unnoticed. Free market ideology made a comeback. In

1947 Congress passed the Taft-Hartley Act, which decreed that a worker is entitled to the benefits that unions generate for workers regardless of whether the worker is a union member. (That some workers are still union members is testimony to how irrational some of them can be.) And at the University of Chicago, the economist Don Patinkin renewed the claim that low wages would restore an economy to full employment, no matter how depressed that economy is.

Patinkin granted Keynes his theory of investment, "animal spirit" included. But he revived an objection to Keynes's theory first raised by Keynes's colleague at Cambridge, Arthur Pigou. When investors are stuck in a pessimistic mood and employment declines, Pigou and then Patinkin argued, the economy will be restored to full employment by an increase in consumption. What Keynes failed to see, according to Pigou and Patinkin, is that consumers base their decision on how much to consume not only on how much real income they earn, but also on the level of prices. Consumers hold some cash, Pigou and Patinkin argued, and when prices become lower the purchasing power of this cash increases and they consume more. When investment declines prices decline, which causes consumption to increase. As a result full employment is restored.

But Patinkin's argument is incomplete. There is only one asset in the economy whose real value increases when the price of consumer good falls: cash. It is easy to see that what's true for cash is not true for a real asset like a house; when all prices fall by the same proportion the real value of the house does not increase, but rather remains unchanged. When it comes to a financial asset, the effect of a fall in prices is more complicated. It makes the borrower poorer, because she would have to pay back her loan with dollars that would be worth more. And for the same reason it makes the lender richer. The net effect on the demand for consumption from these two countervailing forces—the increase in the real value of the cash that people hold, on the one hand, and the redistribution of wealth from borrowers to lenders, on the other—is impossible to predict. Would a fall in prices necessarily stimulate consumption? And if it does, would it do it with such force that a deep downturn like the Great Depression would be entirely avoided? Pigou, the original developer of this theory, was not sure.[4] But Keynes did not address this question at all. Why? According to Keynes's contemporaries Joan Robinson and Richard Kahn, Keynes thought that the *level* of prices was immaterial. What was material was the fact that prices were *falling*, and because of that consumers would want to delay consumption.[5] In the same vein, the economist Christina Romer, President Obama's chair of the Council of Economic Advisers, explains that, just like investors, consumers also require a certain level of optimism to spend. When prices fall because unemployment is increasing, this fall may have a negative effect on consumers' confidence, and it may lead them to believe that they need to save more and consume less. Furthermore, when prices fall, consumers may cut their consumption rather than increase it, to take advantage of even lower prices in the future.[6]

During the first years of the Great Depression, prices fell substantially. They fell 2 percent in 1929 (Black Tuesday was on October 30, which means that the decline occurred over just two months), 9 percent in 1930, 10 percent in 1931, and 5 percent in 1932.[7] Yet employment did not recover. Why? First, for all the reasons that were discussed above, falling prices do not necessarily lead to an increase in the demand for consumer goods. More important, though, an increase in the demand for consumer goods simply cannot serve as a substitute for the loss of investors' optimism. Workers work with capital goods; therefore when they lose their jobs, capital goods "lose their jobs" too, and disinvestment takes place. When workers are hired, capital goods must be "hired" too, and investment takes place. Therefore no increase in employment can occur as long as investors persist in their pessimism and refuse to invest. Keynes was right to focus on the decrease in demand for investment goods as the cause of unemployment. The case of car production during the Great Depression shows this most clearly.

CAR PRODUCTION, 1929–35

The relationship between consumption and investment can be gleaned from the research of economists Timothy Bresnahan and Daniel Raff about the car industry during the Great Depression. Bresnahan and Raff discovered that when employment in the years 1929–33 declined, not only workers but also the capital goods that they work with "lost their jobs." Of 211 plants open in 1929, one-half, or 105 plants, were closed in 1933. When production in the industry started to increase again in the years 1933–35, the factories that closed did not reopen. Large-scale investment took place instead: the plants that never closed bought new machinery, thus increasing their installed horsepower by 25 percent; and in addition, sixteen entirely new plants opened as well.[8]

What made investors regain their confidence in the car industry after 1933? We cannot be sure, but it should be noted that between 1933 and 1935 the average price of a car increased by 2.5 percent. This is, of course, a small increase, but it came despite the fact the number of vehicles produced more than doubled during this period. It appears that when investors regained their optimism, they went overboard. The fact that between 1933 and 1935 wages in the car industry increased by 27 percent is another indication of excess optimism.

14.

"STICKY WAGES"

Keynes explained that the level of employment in the economy is determined by the aggregate demand for goods and services, and not by the level of wages, whether nominal or real. But contemporary economists, even those who describe themselves as Keynesians, strongly disagree. According to them, the level of wages is precisely what determines the level of employment (and therefore of unemployment). During the Depression, they argue, wages were too high. Had they been sufficiently lower, the level of employment would have been higher.[1] Why is the opposition to Keynes's theory so strong? Not because it was tested empirically and found wrong, but because of the conclusions that follow from the recognition that lower wages cannot eliminate unemployment. The first conclusion is that the free market system is not self-adjusting and that therefore the government should intervene and regulate the economy. The second conclusion is that the VMP theory of wages is wrong and, therefore, so is the claim that workers get paid what "they are worth." Economists therefore set out to develop theories to prove that wages are sticky in general, and that sticky wages caused the Great Depression.

There are two theories of why wages are sticky. The best known among the authors of the first theory is Milton Friedman, and the conclusion from this theory, drawn by economists Robert Lucas and

Leonard Rapping, is that when workers are unemployed it is not because there are no jobs available but because they are unwilling to work for the prevailing wages. That means that unemployment is always, including during the Great Depression, "voluntary," and therefore there is nothing the government can do about it.

The most famous economist among the authors of the second theory is Joseph Stiglitz, and the conclusion from this theory is that unemployment is actually efficient, because it instills fear in the hearts of the workers who do have jobs. Fear is necessary to prevent workers from shirking their responsibility to work hard. We shall see that in this theory unemployment is involuntary. (This means that the unemployed are unable to find work even though they are willing to work at or slightly below the market wage.) The government should nevertheless not intervene to reduce unemployment; if it did, shirking would increase.

The causes of unemployment in the two theories are very different, but about whom is to blame for unemployment the two theories are in total agreement: unemployment is the fault of workers. According to Friedman, workers are unemployed because they refuse to accept the wages that are offered to them. According to Stiglitz, they are unemployed because they are shirkers who require the discipline imposed by the threat of unemployment.

FRIEDMAN: UNEMPLOYMENT IS THE FAULT OF MISINFORMED WORKERS

Milton Friedman's theory of why wages are sticky was also developed independently by the economist Edmund Phelps. The theory, which we shall call the "misinformed workers" theory of unemployment, is as follows. Suppose that the demand for goods and services in the economy falls, and that as a consequence prices also fall. When the price of a good falls, the Value of the Marginal Product of the workers who produce the good falls with it. In response, employers want to lower their workers' wages. But some of the workers may be unaware that all prices in the economy have fallen. These workers believe instead that only the price of the good that they produce has fallen, and they therefore quit their jobs to look for higher-paying jobs with other employers.[2] It is thus the erroneous belief of workers that they can get higher wages elsewhere that is responsible for their own unemployment.

This situation is depicted in figure 14.1. In the figure, the price of a Big Mac falls from $3 to $2 a unit and this results in a lower VMP curve (the marginal product itself has not changed, but with a lower price the value of the marginal product is lower). McDonald's wishes to lower the wage

FIGURE 14.1: STICKY WAGES WHEN WORKERS ARE MISINFORMED

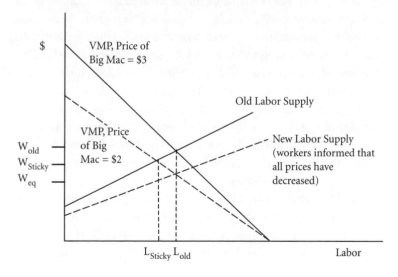

to $W_{eq(uilibrium)}$ and to continue to employ L_{old} workers. But in response some workers quit and become unemployed while looking for higher-paid work elsewhere. With a lower VMP curve and an unchanged supply of labor curve, the wage is W_{Sticky} instead of W_{eq}, and this is the sense in which the wage is "sticky." As a result the level of employment decreases from L_{old} to L_{Sticky}. Had the workers been informed that all prices in the economy had fallen, their supply of labor would have shifted to the dashed labor supply in the diagram, and as a result the wage would have been W_{eq} and there would have been no unemployment.

The economists Robert Lucas and Leonard Rapping applied Friedman's theory of sticky wages to explain unemployment during the Great Depression and argued that even that unemployment was all "voluntary."[3] According to this theory factories during the Great Depression closed because when the prices of goods started to fall, some of their workers believed that only the prices of the goods that *they* were producing fell; they quit their jobs to look for better-paying ones. Unemployed workers who were looking for jobs turned down these newly vacated jobs also, because they shared the same misinformation and also waited for better offers. According to Lucas and Rapping, "In our model . . . the current wage is assumed to equate quantity demanded and quantity supplied exactly each period."[4] When the quantity supplied is equal to the quantity demanded, any worker who is willing to work at the market wage rate always has a job. The workers who are not working are those who would agree to work only for a higher wage (according to Friedman, because they believe, erroneously, that if they keep searching for higher-paying jobs they will find them).

The only problem with this argument is that it requires the workers' misinformation about wages to last a very long time. The Great Depression continued for many years, leading the economist Albert Rees to ask: "How long does it take workers to revise their expectations of normal wages in light of the facts? Unemployment was never below 14 percent of the labor force between 1931 and 1939, and was still 17 percent of the labor force in 1939, a decade after the depression began."[5] In other words, the claim that the Great Depression was caused by the failure of workers to recognize that there was a Great Depression does not make sense. But this is the only explanation that Friedman's theory of unemployment offers.

President Reagan made frequent use of Friedman's and Lucas's claim that unemployment is voluntary. Following a revolution that deposed the shah of Iran in 1979, oil prices increased and unemployment increased with them. In 1982, when the rate of unemployment was 9.7 percent, Reagan remarked that the Sunday issue of the *New York Times* listed 44.5 pages of help-wanted ads, the *Washington Post* listed 33.5 pages, and the *Los Angeles Times* listed 65.5 pages. He famously asked, "How does a person . . . justify calling themselves unemployed when there's a fellow spending money advertising and saying, 'I've got a job; come fill my job'?"[6] Reagan repeated such stories throughout his presidency, but at times he was challenged. At a news conference a reporter noted that there were four thousand applicants for three hundred openings at a hotel on Long Island and asked how this fit within Reagan's claim that unemployment was voluntary. The president replied that some of the wanted ads require skills that did not match those of the unemployed.[7] This was, of course, correct but not necessarily consistent with the theory that the unemployed don't want to work. There was no follow-up question, though. The claim that the unemployed don't want to work gained respectability, and the view that welfare recipients were lazy replaced the view that the market economy was not producing enough jobs. When President Clinton came to office, welfare recipients were forced to work for their welfare checks. The fact that they agreed gives the lie both to the claim that unemployment is voluntary and that these workers are unfit to work.

Surely those who are working for a welfare check would agree to work at a higher-paying regular job. But nobody has noticed. Because of the hard and reliable work these people do, local governments now exploit them as cheap labor that they use to replace regular employees. In New York, for example, more than six thousand welfare recipients help maintain the city's parks.[8] The union of the municipal employees sued the city but lost, because the judge believed that welfare workers should do "real jobs."[9] The jobs they do are, of course, real, but they do not pay wages that the workers can live on. Reagan's question should therefore be reversed: how does a government justify forcing people to work for welfare benefits instead of a living wage?

WHAT ABOUT THOSE LONG LINES?

Regardless of one's theory of the causes of the Great Depression, one puzzle remains: When four thousand workers apply for two hundred jobs at any period of time (figure 14.2) why doesn't the wage drop to such a low level that only two hundred workers would be interested and there would be no line? Isn't that proof that the unemployment of these workers is voluntary?

When workers are desperate, a lower wage does not necessarily make the line of job applicants shorter.[10] The workers who work for welfare checks are proof that there is no wage sufficiently small or humiliation sufficiently deep to stop desperate people from seeking work. The puzzle is, therefore, not a puzzle at all. A different question that may be asked, however, is why the wage isn't always driven to the minimum possible level. Why doesn't the wage always fall to the level of the welfare check when there are many workers on the welfare rolls? Smith and Ricardo were also puzzled by this question, and their only answer was to invoke

FIGURE 14.2: FOUR THOUSAND JOBLESS, TWO HUNDRED JOBS, 2006

Credit: Andrea Mohin, *The New York Times*/Redux

"habit and custom." We cannot solve the puzzle here, but perhaps we can attempt a fuller answer nevertheless.

Economist Richard Thaler noted that in 1992, when Florida was caught with limited disaster-protection supplies when Hurricane Andrew struck, Home Depot did not raise its prices.[11] Why? A higher price for plywood would not have resulted in more plywood being available, and raising the price under this condition would have been exploitation. We will never know whether Home Depot kept its old prices out of decency or out of fear of consumer retaliation. What matters is that it did. It appears that a similar situation exists in the labor market. When workers and employers know that a lower wage will not create more jobs, workers do not undercut each other, and employers do not reduce wages.

An example of how responsive wages are when they *can* produce more jobs comes from the automobile industry in 2007. Delphi, the main parts supplier to General Motors, threatened to close all its plants in the United States unless the workers agreed to significantly lower wages. In response the workers agreed to a 40 percent wage decrease, from $27.44/hour to $16.23/hour. It is interesting that the workers agreed to this wage cut even though it would not save all the jobs; Delphi nevertheless still planned to close twenty-one of its twenty-eight plants.[12]

15

"EFFICIENCY WAGES" OR: WHY UNEMPLOYMENT
IS THE FAULT OF SHIRKING BY WORKERS

As was already mentioned, the efficiency wage theory, developed by Joseph Stiglitz, starts from the assumption that given the opportunity, workers will not work as hard as they should. Detecting workers' shirking is costly and, therefore, instead of increasing the probability of detection, employers choose to increase the severity of the penalty on a shirker who is caught. The most severe penalty that an employer can inflict is firing a worker. But if a worker who gets fired could easily find another job that paid exactly the same wage, getting fired would not be a deterrent. The employer therefore tries to pay her workers a wage that is higher than the wage that other employers pay. Stiglitz calls this high wage the "efficiency wage" because it reduces shirking and increases the work effort. With the efficiency wage in place, a worker would have something to lose from getting fired.

It may appear that the efficiency wage plan is bound to fail. If all employers pay the "efficiency wage," why should a worker worry about getting fired? She would earn this wage when she is rehired by another employer. Stiglitz invokes the VMP theory to close this hole in the theory. Recall that according to the neo-classical theory there is a "law of the diminishing productivity of labor," and that therefore an employer who pays a high wage must hire fewer employees. But when all employers hire fewer employees this creates persistent unemployment, and it is the fear of joining the ranks of the unemployed that keeps workers from shirking.

In Stiglitz's theory the unemployed are not workers who have been fired from their jobs because they shirked. Unemployment exists because employers deliberately pay a wage that is higher than the wage that workers would agree to work for. Workers who don't have jobs are just as diligent as workers who do, but employers do not hire them for a lower wage because if they were to work for a lower wage they may shirk. According to Stiglitz, this is the explanation for periods of high and persistent unemployment. The 25 percent unemployment rate during the Great Depression and the 10 percent unemployment rate in the period of 1979–82 were due to the fear of shirking by workers.[1]

The efficiency wage theory of unemployment makes four claims. The first is that shirking by workers is ubiquitous; employers would not want to pay all workers do-not-shirk premiums if only a few shirk. The second is that do-not-shirk-premiums actually prevent shirking. The third is that workers are in fact paid do-not-shirk premiums. The fourth is that these premiums lead to unemployment. What is the evidence regarding these claims?

The first and the second claims are offered without any evidence at all. As evidence for the third, the economists Dominique Goux and Eric Maurin present data that workers earn more when they work for larger firms. Goux and Maurin argue that the wage differences that they discovered must be due to do-not-shirk premiums.[2] Why? Because they have ruled out all other possible explanations, such as quality of labor or the location of the firm. And why would larger firms pay higher premiums? Goux and Maurin claim that in larger firms it is easier for workers to shirk.

Goux's and Maurin's own findings cast doubt, however, on this interpretation of their results. In their study they controlled for workers' occupation, yet they did not find that this made a difference; firms that pay higher wages in one occupation pay higher wages in all occupations. But as the economists William Dickens and Lawrence Katz observed, while a particular occupation in a firm may provide an opportunity for shirking, there is no reason why all occupations within that industry would suffer from the same problem.[3] Their evidence is therefore actually inconsistent with the efficiency wage theory.

In addition, their interpretation of the results suffers from a fundamental, perhaps fatal, problem. Why should wage differences lead us to invoke shirking? Goux and Maurin present us with a false dichotomy. There may be other reasons for wage dispersion than the ones that Goux and Maurin considered, and, therefore, shirking is not the only alternative. One reason why large firms pay high wages to all their workers may be that such firms have large numbers of shareholders and the managers who negotiate employees' wages are therefore the least supervised. Instead of serving as an incentive to reduce shirking, the high wages that such a firm pays may be a form of shirking itself. Goux and Maurin also found that wages are higher in capital intensive firms. In such firms workers have a greater opportunity to disrupt the workflow, and the higher wages that they earn may simply reflect their greater bargaining power.[4] The evidence that employers pay do-not-shirk premiums is feeble.

Like the first and the second claim, the fourth claim—that the payment of efficiency wages creates unemployment—is also offered without evidence at all (so much for the science of economics). The "law of the diminishing marginal productivity of labor" is invoked instead, since it makes it necessary to hire fewer workers when the wage is higher. The economists Alan Krueger and Lawrence Summers state: "The demonstration of important inter-industry wage differentials . . . creates a *prima facie* case for the existence of involuntary unemployment."[5] In other words, firms that pay efficiency wages must be deliberately understaffed. The problem with this argument is that production is carried out by teams, and it is therefore hard to imagine how understaffing can actually take place. This is especially so since it is the larger and more capital-intensive firms that pay the highest do-not-shirk premiums, and they are therefore the ones that should suffer from the greatest understaffing. How can this be when production processes that involve more machines and more workers are probably less flexible in terms of the staffing that they require? Without evidence, the claim that firms deliberately hire fewer employees than their production processes require should not be accepted.

But even if workers were paid premiums not to shirk, and even if these premiums were creating unemployment, it is still unclear how this would lead to an increase in the rate of unemployment that then persists over several years. Stiglitz claims that efficiency wages were responsible for the unemployment during the Great Depression and the recession of 1979–82, but it is hard to see how. George Akerlof and Janet Yellen, who also contributed to the development of the efficiency wage theory (Akerlof shared the Nobel Prize with Stiglitz), explain that an employer is reluctant to lower the wages of her workers even when the demand for her product declines because workers shirk when they believe that the wage they are paid is unfairly low. "What if my workers do not know that the demand for my product has declined and start shirking?" is the employer's reasoning, according to Yellen's and Akerlof's theory.[6] Misinformation is the cause of unemployment in either case, however, and Rees's critique of Friedman's and Lucas's theory applies equally here: how long does it take workers to realize, and how long does it take employers to realize that their workers have realized that there is a recession? As the subprime recession shows, employers do not shy away from cutting wages and jobs all at the same time.

The claim that a large proportion of workers would shirk unless paid do-not-shirk premiums was presented without any evidence, but this did not stop the economist Sam Bowles from proposing a better solution to the ostensible problem of shirking than the "efficiency wage": not because the efficiency wage does not work, but because the efficiency wage, according to the VMP theory, creates unemployment. Bowles's solution would permit employers to pay their workers a lower wage without this wage leading to more shirking. And what is this solution? Socialism. In a socialist system workers own the factory in which they work, and therefore they would shirk less to begin with, and if they do shirk, then their coworkers would turn them in:

> A more democratic structure of decision making and a more egalitarian distribution of the firm's net revenues, for example, might both reduce the incentive to pursue nonwork activities and heighten the cost of so doing by enlisting fellow workers as more ardent enforcers of the pace of work, or more willing cooperators with the surveillance system.[67]

The editors of the journal of the American Economic Association recognized the significance of an article by a self-proclaimed socialist who blames unemployment on shirking by workers, and made it the lead article of the *American Economic Review* in 1985.

EFFICIENCY WAGES AND FORD'S $5 DAY

On January 5, 1914, Henry Ford announced that he would raise the wage of his workers from $2.34/day to $5.00/day. This was twice the going wage and it generated the line shown in Figure 15.1.

For Krueger and Summers this is a clear example of the efficiency

FIGURE 15.1: THE $5 DAY

'GOLD RUSH'
IS STARTED
BY FORD'S
$5 OFFER

Thousands of Men Seek Employment in Detroit Factory.

Will Distribute $10,000,000 in Semi-Monthly Bonuses.

No Employe to Receive Less Than Five Dollars a Day.

wage theory at work. Why else would Ford double the wage if not to elicit harder work from its workers? But economic historian Daniel Raff could not find any evidence to support this claim when he examined the actual operation of Ford's factory.[8] The workers who received the new wage worked in a new factory with a new and revolutionary method of production: the assembly line. On the assembly line the opportunity to shirk simply did not exist. Raff then investigated whether the high wages were intended to decrease the turnover rate of workers at the factory. In 1913 Ford had a turnover rate of 370 percent: it employed 13,623 workers daily, but during the year 39,575 workers resigned (and a few thousand more were fired). High as the turnover was, Raff discovered that it did not pose a problem to Ford because replacing workers was easy. In fact, in 1914 a Ford supervisor bragged about how easy it was:

> If an immigrant who has never even seen the inside of a foundry before cannot be made a first-class molder of one piece only in three days, he can never be any use to us on the floor; and two days is held to be ample time to make a first-class core molder of a man who has never before seen a core-molding bench in his life.[9]

Turnover rates did decrease by two-thirds between 1913 and 1914, the year that the $5 wage went into effect, but they declined by the same proportion in all factories in the region over that period, not just at Ford's.

Let's suppose, however, that the $5 wage was an efficiency wage. Suppose that it did reduce shirking or was the reason that turnover declined. Did this high wage create involuntary unemployment? Did Ford place fewer employees on the assembly line than were required to man it? In 1914, the year of the new wage, daily employment at Ford fell by 1,500. But in the following year it increased by 6,000 employees, an increase of about 50 percent from the figure for 1913! According to Raff, Ford increased its wage at that particular time because it was introducing the assembly line. This technology, according to Raff, made Ford more vulnerable to strike action; with the higher wage it was trying to buy industrial peace. This may be, but the fact that Ford was substantially increasing its workforce cannot be ignored. As we know from the high turnover rate, in 1913 the labor market was tight; finding a large number of new workers under such conditions required a large premium. What the premium did not do, however, is cause Ford to employ *fewer* workers. Ford's $5/day clearly does not support the claim (of Friedman, Lucas, Stiglitz, Akerlof, Krueger and Summers) that unemployment is the result of high wages.

16

EXECUTIVE COMPENSATION

As Figure 16.1 shows, since 1990 CEOs' compensation has been growing many folds faster than corporate profits (and workers' wages). It is no wonder, then, that the claim that executive compensation can be explained by executive productivity has met with incredulity, and that in 2006, when the compensation of Hank McKinnell, the CEO of Pfizer, was challenged by shareholders (see Chapter 13), this became news.

The source of CEOs' ability to take advantage of shareholders was identified as far back as 1932, in *The Modern Corporation and Private Property* by the economists Adolf Berle and Gardiner Means. The ownership of a corporation is diffused among a large number of shareholders, the book explained, and there is nobody to mind the store. The bargaining power of a CEO of a large corporation is practically limitless. Is this a problem, though? A theoretical treatment of this question was developed by the economists Michael Jensen and William Meckling in 1976, and their answer is that corporations are not run as well as they theoretically could be, but that shareholders are not being taken advantage of.

Perhaps the best way to understand Jansen and Meckling's analysis is to start with the origin of a corporation. Think of an inventor who is so successful that her invention brings her profits of $100 million a year after the salary that she pays herself for running her company. Assume

FIGURE 16.1: EXECUTIVE COMPENSATION,
PROFITS, AND WAGES

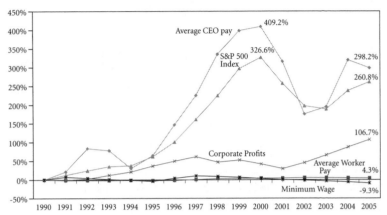

Source: Sarah Anderson and John Cavanagh (Institute for Policy Studies), Chuck Collins and Eric Benjamin (United for a Fair Economy), "Executive Excess 2006": http://www.faireconomy.org/files/ExecutiveExcess2006.pdf

also that this stream of profits would continue forever. After a few years in business the inventor wishes to sell her company. Because there aren't many buyers who can afford to buy the whole company for themselves, the inventor issues one million stocks and sells them to one million buyers who each buy one share. Suppose that investments in the economy normally earn a return of 10 percent a year. What will be the total value that the inventor would get for her company?

We may imagine that the total value of these stocks would be $1 billion, because this is the sum that needs to be invested to generate an interest payment of $100 million a year when the rate of interest is 10 percent. (At the end of each year the interest is withdrawn and the principal is redeposited for an additional year.) But in fact it would be lower. The reason has to do with the ownership structure of a corporation.

One million owners cannot all run the corporation at the same time. What they will do instead is hire a CEO to run the company on their behalf. The CEO will probably consume wasteful perks (a problem discussed in the first part of this book), but here we concentrate only on the problem of her compensation. Suppose that initially the CEO's salary is set at the level that the original inventor used to pay herself, but that after she is hired she increases her own salary by $1 million. Will the shareholders get together and fire the CEO? Chances are that most of them will not even be aware that the pay raise has taken place. Why should they, when each shareholder's loss is only $1? Even if the loss to each owner were more substantial, organizing opposition to the CEO would be costly, and often more trouble than it's worth to the individual shareholder.

Formally, executive salaries are determined not by the executives themselves but by boards of directors. The question is, therefore, who will discipline the CEO and the directors who approve her exorbitant salary? Corporate board memberships are coveted positions: in 2001, shareholders paid directors in the largest two hundred corporations an average of $153,000; the directors of Enron were paid $380,000 annually. Savvy businesspeople that they are, the directors know that, while it is the shareholders who pay them, in most cases the only candidates for directorships are those nominated not by shareholders but by the CEOs themselves.[1]

But, Jansen and Meckling explain, nobody gets cheated. People who buy the company's shares are well aware of the possibility of these shenanigans. Instead of paying $1,000 per share, they would agree to pay, say, only $500 per share. As a result, the total market value of the corporation will be only $500 million, not $1 billion. The shenanigans and high compensation of the CEO are capitalized into the price of the stock, and the original inventor will suffer all the consequences from her decision to split the ownership among many individuals.

Jansen and Meckling call the problems that arise from the fractured ownership of a corporation the "agency problem," because the corporation is not run by a single owner but by a CEO who is the owners' agent. Their theory is known as the "agency theory."

While a CEO rarely has to answer to shareholders, it is often argued that she does have to answer to "corporate raiders," who threaten to perform a "hostile takeover" and fire her if she exploits the shareholders. According to this argument, raiders keep CEOs and corporate directors honest. What is the incentive of the raider in all this? Why would she want to fulfill this role? Once the bad CEO and board are replaced by a good CEO and board, the price of the stock will increase, and the raider would thus be compensated for her efforts.

This argument suffers, of course, from a critical logical flaw, because once the raider sells her shares the corporation will be mismanaged once again. The price of the stock will therefore be high only as long as the raider owns it. In addition, raiders are actually a source of yet another shareholders' loss, because to protect themselves against the raider, a CEO and his board may squander the corporation's profits even further.

The prize for costly raids goes to Ross Perot. In 1986 Perot prepared the grounds for a hostile takeover of GM by buying .8 percent of the outstanding stocks, and leveraging this position to become a director of the company.[2] There was very little about GM that Perot liked. The company was procedure-oriented instead of results-oriented, senior management ate in a corporate dining room that isolated them from workers, and, most important, the board of directors sided with management and betrayed shareholders. Shareholders own the company, Perot told reporters: "We must make it clear that the management serves at the pleasure of the shareholders. . . . The managers of mature corporations with no concentration of owners have gotten themselves into the position of effectively selecting the board members who will represent the stockholders. . . . Is the board a rubber stamp for Roger [Smith, the CEO]? Hell, no! We'd have to upgrade it to be a rubber stamp."[3]

So what did Perot do about it? Did he organize a stockholders' meeting to get rid of the CEO and the directors who collaborated with him? He did something far better! He made the board pay him $346.8 million of shareholders' money to go away. (The board gave Perot $742.8 million, although the market value of his shares was $396 million.) He also signed an agreement that prohibited him from criticizing GM, under penalty of $7.5 million. But what he could not do is deny that he was receiving stolen money. So Perot expressed revulsion at his own theft: "Is spending all this money the highest and best use of GM's capital? . . . I want to give the directors a chance to do the right thing. It is incomprehensible to me that they would want to spend $750 million on this."[4] This did not stop him from taking the money though, and he kept his mouth shut so as not to risk the $7.5 million. And when GM's CEO Roger Smith (infamous from Michael Moore's documentary *Roger & Me*) retired four years later, the board doubled his retirement package to $1.2 million annually.[5]

Perot used money, not a gun, to threaten Roger Smith, which is why this type of holdup is called "greenmail." In addition to paying off greenmailers, CEOs sometimes defend themselves by creating "poison pills," corporate rules that make it unprofitable for any investor to take over the corporation no matter how badly it is run, and by including "golden parachutes" in their employment contracts that amount to large payoffs in the event of a takeover. What's common to all these devices is that they break any links between executive compensation and performance.

Is it true that shareholders correctly anticipate CEO and board behavior and therefore are unharmed by it? It was not true for the employees of Enron, who were lured by the company's CEO and executives into investing their life savings in the shares of "their" company and lost everything they had; the employees were also unaware that the executives were selling their own shares at the same time they were encouraging their employees to buy more of them. And it was not true for the Pfizer shareholder who was surprised by McKinnell's exorbitant compensation given his poor performance. Even Congress was blindsided by the lack of relationship between CEO compensation and performance. When in 2007 Stanley O'Neal, the CEO of Merrill Lynch, was "forced" to retire with a retirement package of $160 million after the company had lost $8 billion because of the investment strategy he had devised, Congress ordered O'Neal and the chair of the board to testify before its finance committee. What puzzled Rep. Henry Waxman and the newspapers that covered this issue was that O'Neal had a contract that did not contain any provisions for reducing his pay in case of poor performance on his part. As figure 16.1 shows, increases in executive pay that could not be justified by increases in profits did not afflict only Pfizer or Merrill Lynch. Without a rational relationship between profits and compensation, how could shareholders predict what this relationship would be? Jansen and Meckling's assurance that shareholders are not harmed by "agency costs" is not borne out by the evidence.

The economists Xavier Gabaix and Augustin Landier discovered that the compensation of an executive increases with the market value (capitalization) of the corporation she runs.[6] Thus, not only is executive compensation unjustifiably high, it also gives executives an incentive to increase the market value of their corporation regardless of whether this is good for profits. With Berle and Means's theory, this is easy to understand. When a CEO takes $100 million in compensation and the value of the company is $100 million, the cost per $1 shareholders' equity is $1.

But when the value of the corporation is $100 billion, the cost per dollar of shareholder's equity is only one-tenth of a cent. To escape shareholders' vigilance in small corporations, executives engage in mergers and acquisitions regardless of whether these will increase profits. According to "Parkinson's Law," a bureaucrat always wants to hire two additional bureaucrats who would report to her. In corporations the problem is even bigger, because in addition to prestige, executives have a monetary incentive to create Leviathans.

WAGES, EXECUTIVE COMPENSATION, PROFITS, AND TEAM PRODUCTION

Because production is carried out by teams, an individual's contribution to production, whether she is a worker, a manager, or even a piece of machinery, cannot be separated from the contribution of all the rest of her teammates. The division of a product among those who produced it therefore cannot be determined by the process of production itself. Who then decides how the product should be divided between those who produced it? And how do they make this decision? Currently, executives are the ones who decide who gets how much, and they take the lion's share for themselves; workers and shareholders are almost powerless. But this is not preordained. The source of the executives' power lies in the fact that the ownership of corporations is diffused among many individuals. This is an inherent characteristic of large-scale production and cannot be changed. What can be changed, however, is whether executives are permitted to turn it into an advantage. It is the role of government to make sure that one person not exploit another, and, therefore, to determine the maximum ratio between the highest compensation of an executive and the lowest wage of a worker, and between the earnings of shareholders and total payments of labor. What should these ratios be?

What's fair should be determined by the political process and then written into law.

Arguably, the damage from the teaching of the economist's theory of wages is far greater than the damage from the teaching of creationism. Yet the theory of wages is part of economics education in any and all schools, and it continues without any notice or opposition. The reason is, of course, not hard to understand. While everyone is hurt when we teach religion and pretend it's science, not everyone is hurt when we teach economics. What workers lose, executives and capitalists gain; and it is the latter who study economics, hire economists, and endow schools.

The battle for a fair distribution of the product that we all produce together has so far been waged in the workplace and in the political arena. It must also be fought in the classroom, however, because it is there that the lie that "workers are paid what they deserve" is taught.

AFTERWORD

According to the tenets of economics, what's good for the economy is what is good for the rich and powerful. All of us are being held hostage to a pseudoscience that perpetuates two powerful myths: the first is that economic efficiency can and should be separated from economic equity, and that any policy that would shift any of society's resources from the wealthy to the poor is "inefficient." The second is that what a person earns, be it the meager wage of an hourly worker or the astronomical compensation of an executive, is simply the value of the product that she has produced.

As I hope this book has shown, the attacks by contemporary economists on classical theories of redistribution and wages are lacking in both theoretical merit and humanity. When used as the rationale for abolishing food subsidies in Indonesia during a food crisis or as the basis for lowering environmental standards in the Third World, neo-classical economic theories lead to hunger and death. In the United States, these theories of efficiency and wages are directly and indirectly responsible for many unhappy aspects of American life: millions of high school–aged teenagers must work to help support their families, yet we do not pay child subsidies; millions of old people must continue to work because the average Social Security payment is far below the poverty line, yet high incomes are exempt from the Social Security tax; millions of young people do not attend college at all because they cannot afford it and millions of others must work while they do, yet tuition in public colleges has increased four times faster than the level of median income since 1980.

Whenever a social or economic policy that will serve the needs of ordinary people surfaces, we can be sure to find an economist standing by, poised to ask, "But is it good for the economy?" (As if "the economy" were some entity different from the best interests of the general populace.) Since most policies require taxes to fund them, we are also told that taxes themselves are "bad for the economy." But, as we have seen, there is no evidence that taxes do any harm at all to the economy; in fact, the economy grew just as fast when, during the years 1948–81, the highest tax rates were often twice their level today.

One of the main reasons that redistributive policies—from progressive taxes to rent control to food subsidies to Medicaid—are necessary in the first place is that modern economists have successfully sold the United States on their version of wage theory, in which workers do not earn enough to live on and executives earn obscene amounts. The ratio between an average worker's pay and an average executive's compensation is currently one to four hundred, or worse. But, as this book has shown, the claim that a person earns an amount determined by the value of what she produces is fundamentally flawed; production is carried out by teams, and the product of one member cannot be separated from the product of the whole team. Despite modern economists' arguments to the contrary, the evidence shows that wages are determined by the power workers possess (or fail to possess) at the bargaining table. Classical economists recognized the relationship of wages to power more than two hundred years ago, before it was intentionally obfuscated by John Bates Clark and his neo-classical followers.

The remedy for the rule of power is the rule of law. New laws must be developed to check the unfair distribution of the fruits of our labor. One such law would set a maximum ratio at any given company between the highest executive compensation and the lowest worker's wage. Another would set a maximum ratio for the division of income between labor and corporate owners or shareholders. And a third new law would raise the minimum wage and tie it to the median wage, which would have the effect of making the minimum wage a consistent living wage.

Would executives agree to work for compensation lower than what they currently earn? We have seen that work effort is independent of the level of executive compensation; drastic cuts in the highest marginal tax rate following the election of President Reagan in 1980 did not cause executives to work more. What lower compensation will do, however, is lower the ability of executives to consume excessively. From apartments that are too large to private ranches and beaches that gobble up open space to doctors who promise to treat only a few wealthy patients, executives take more than their fair share and leave too little for the rest of us, while threatening our health to boot.

If social policies that pull children, college students, and old people out of the workforce are enacted, our current per capita GDP of $47,000 might decline, perhaps by as much as 10 percent. But with a GDP per capita of "only" $42,000 and new policies governing the distribution of our collective wealth, each family of four could have resources worth $168,000 a year. With such abundance, giving every child a childhood, every qualified young person a college education, and every senior the chance to retire would leave plenty of money to spare.

The economy is us, and we are not doing well. We need to turn economics from a weapon that is being used against us into a science that will show us how we can do better.

ACKNOWLEDGMENTS

Many people contributed to this book. My friend and colleague Tom Russell read both the whole manuscript and many pieces of it many times, and his criticisms—which were just as many—were always constructive. I greatly appreciated and enjoyed the many hours he spent discussing the book with me. My friends and colleagues Panos Mavrokefalos and Uri Ronnen could also be counted on to read and improve any part-in-progress that was sent to them.

Mike Merrill, dean of the Van Arsdale Center for Labor Studies, was always encouraging. In addition, Simon Kawitzki, Larry Michelotti, Kerim Odekon, and Steve Sheffrin read the manuscript and made many helpful comments.

At The New Press, Diane Wachtell was as thorough and careful an editor as anyone could hope to have. Diane reorganized the manuscript and insisted that every argument make sense to a comparative literature major like herself—a high standard indeed. Managing editor Maury Botton and copy editor Nick Taylor were extremely helpful.

This book would not have been written if not for Colin Robinson, who first signed the book up at The New Press.

The issues the book grapples with were discussed often around the dinner table at my parents' home, and they and my sister, Yael Weinman, influenced my thinking greatly. At a crucial moment when I was in graduate school, my cousin, Sy Adler, asked me whether I wanted to be rich or to complete my Ph.D. Thank you Sy.

My wife Ellen provided not only essential encouragement and moral support, but also invaluable editorial help. She read each part of the book just as soon as it was written—and rewritten—and her contributions are present on every page. The book also benefitted greatly from discussions with my students at Columbia, Pratt, and the Van Arsdale Center for Labor Studies, and I am thankful to them for exploring these ideas with me.

I gratefully acknowledge support from the Kelber Fund of the Empire State College Foundation. I also thank Len Munnik for letting me use his drawing from *The Tale of the Turnip* and Michael Reeve for his photograph of Jeremy Bentham.

Last but not least, my daughter Lily enjoys all book parties, and has been waiting for mine for far too long. I thank her for her patience.

NOTES

1. Income Equality

1. Pope Leo, "*Rerum Novarum*: Encyclical on Capital and Labor," 1891, The Vatican, sixth paragraph, http://www.vatican.va/holy_father/leo_xiii/encyc licals/documents/hf_1-xiii_enc_15051891_rerum-novarum_en.html (accessed June 29, 2009).
2. Vilfredo Pareto, *Manual of Political Economy*, trans. Ann S. Schwier, ed. Ann S. Schwier and Alfred N. Page (New York, A. M. Kelley, 1971), 93.
3. Ibid., 48.
4. Jeremy Bentham, *Principles of the Civil Code*, Part 1 (Oxford: Clarendon Press, 1789), chap. 6, http://www.laits.utexas.edu/poltheory/bentham/pcc/ pcc.pa01.c06.html, (accessed June 29, 2009).
5. A. P. Lerner, *The Economics of Control: Principles of Welfare Economics* (New York: Macmillan, 1944), cited in Gonçalo L. Fonseca, "The Paretian System," The History of Economic Thought Web site, http://cepa.newschool.edu/ het/essays/paretian/paretosocial.htm (accessed June 29, 2009).

2. Equality Does Not Matter

1. The example is adapted from Hal Varian, *Intermediate Microeconomics* (New York: Norton, 2005).
2. We also assume that apartments can be occupied and vacated costlessly and without any friction: landlords can evict tenants at will and without giving them prior notice, and in the same manner tenants can leave their

apartments at will and without prior notice. This assumption is unrealistic, but for an understanding of Pareto efficiency it makes no difference.

3. A more detailed calculation is as follows. To start with, Family G is indifferent between the combinations I and II where:

> I = (city apt., –$1500/month rent);
> II = (suburban apt., –$1,200/month rent).

If family G gets a rent-controlled apartment for which it has to pay only $500/month, then it is indifferent between combinations III and IV where:

> III = (city apt., –$500/month rent)
> IV = (suburban apt., –$1,200/month rent, $1,000 income).

In other words, it is indifferent between living in the rent-controlled apartment and living in the suburbs with an extra income of $1,000/month. If family G sublets the apartment for $4,000/month, its monthly income, after paying the rent of the rent-controlled apartment, is $3,500/month, which is combination V:

> V = (suburban apt., –$1,200/month rent, $3,500 income).

V is preferred to IV, because it contains the same apartment with a higher income. Since IV is equivalent to III, V is preferred to III as well.

4. Our example may appear artificial because it asserts that if a poor family lives in a rent-controlled apartment for which it cannot afford to pay more than $1,500/month, it would agree to sublet if offered any sum above $1,500/month. In reality, even though this family cannot pay more than $1,500/month, it may nevertheless refuse to give it up unless it is paid a much higher sum. It is conceivable that that family would not give up the apartment even for $6,000/month, and in this case rent control is Pareto efficient after all. We will return to this issue in chapter 4. But for the exposition of what Pareto efficiency is, and, more important, for the exposition of how economists apply it in practice, we will assume that a family will always agree to vacate its apartment if offered more than its reservation price.

5. Roy F. Harrod, "Scope and Method of Economics," *Economic Journal* 48, 191 (September, 1938): 397.

6. Nicholas Kaldor, "Welfare Propositions of Economics and Interpersonal Comparisons of Utility," *Economic Journal* 49, 1959 (September 1939): 549–52.

7. John Hicks, "The Foundations of Welfare Economics," *Economic Journal* 9, 195 (September 1939): 696–712; John Hicks, "The Valuation of Social Income," *Economica* 7, 26 (May 1940): 105–24, cited in Fonseca, The History of Economic Thought Web site.

8. U.S. Office of Management and Budget, "Circular A-4," September 17, 2003, http://www.whitehouse.gov/mb/circulars/2004/a-4.pdf.

9. For other problems with cost-benefit analysis, see Frank Ackerman and Lisa Heinzerling, *Priceless: On Knowing the Price of Everything and the Value of Nothing* (New York: The New Press, 2005).

10. Hugh Rockoff, "Price Controls," *Concise Encyclopedia of Economics* (2d ed., 2008), http://www.econlib.org/library/Enc/PriceControls.html (accessed May 26, 2009).

11. *Primetime Live*, February 19, 1997. Transcript is available at http://www.tenant.net/nytenants-announce/nytenants-a-digest.9703 (accessed May 26, 2009).

12. The New York Housing and Vacancy Survey, which is conducted by the Census Bureau every three years, lists only the actual rent paid but not the regulated rent.

13. R. M. Alston, J. R. Kearl, and M. B. Vaughan, "Is There a Consensus Among Economists in the 1990s?" *American Economic Review* 82 (May 1992): 203–9.

14. Walter Block, "Rent Control," *Concise Encyclopedia of Economics* (2d ed., 2008), (accessed May 26, 2009). http://www.econlib.org/library/Enc/Rent-Control.html Some attribute the comparison to Winston Churchill. See "Reality Bites," *Somerville (MA) News*, October 17, 2005, http://somervillenews.typepad.com/the_somerville_news/2005/10/reality_bites_f.html (accessed May 26, 2009).

15. Rent-regulated apartments in New York are either rent stabilized or rent con-
    trolled. The median income of a rent-controlled household was $22,200. See
    New York City Department of Planning, "Housing and Vacancy Control, Ini-
    tial Findings," 2005, http://www.nyc.gov/html/hpd/downloads/pdf/2005
    -Housing-and-vacancy-survey-initial-findings.pdf (accessed May 26, 2009).

3. The Pareto Efficiency Cops

1. Michael Richardson, "Will Suharto Defy the IMF," *International Herald Tribune*, February 16, 1998, http://www.iht.com/articles/1998/02/16/imf.t_2
   .php (accessed May 26, 2009).

2. Paul Blustein, "Rubin says IMF Bailout of Indonesia Is in Danger," *Washington Post*, March 4, 1998.

3. Greg Palast *Journalism and Film*, http://www.gregpalast.com/the-globalizer-
   who-came-in-from-the-cold/ (accessed June 29, 2009).

4. Research by the author shows that 49 percent of full-time retail workers in
   New York City do not have health insurance. Moshe Adler, "Unionization
   and Poverty: The Case of the New York Retail Industry" (working paper 127,
   Economic Policy Institute, Washington DC, December 2003), http://www
   .epinet.org/workingpapers/wp127.pdf.

5. Martin Feldstein, "Rethinking Social Insurance," *American Economic Review*
   95 (March 2005): 10.

6. See: John A. Nyman, *The Theory of Demand for Health Insurance* (Stanford
   Economics and Finance, Stanford, California: Stanford University Press,
   2003). Chapter 3.

7. A. Mark Fendrick and Michael E. Chernew, "Value-based Insurance Design:
   Aligning Incentives to Bridge the Divide Between Quality Improvement and
   Cost Containment," *The American Journal of Managed Care* 12 (December,
   2006): 1–10.

8. Matt Bivens, "Harvard's 'Fitting Choice,' " *The Nation*, June 25, 2001,
   http://www.thenation.com/doc/20010605/bivens.

9. Because of lower wages the cost of controlling pollution in the Third World

may be lower there than it is in the First. But in addition to labor, pollution control also involves inputs that are traded in the world market (e.g., power plants produce less pollution when they burn oil instead of coal). Therefore, while the value of life is proportional to wages, the cost of pollution control is not. If in our example the cost of controlling pollution in the Third World were $3 million instead of $4 million, the result that pollution should not be controlled there would still hold.

10. "Lawrence Summers," *The Whirled Bank Group*, 2001, http://www.whirled bank.org/ourwords/summers.html.

11. Jim Yardley, "China's Next Big Boom Could Be the Foul Air," *New York Times*, October 30, 2005, A1.

4. Why Redistributing Goods May Be Pareto Efficient After All

1. J. K. Horowitz and K. E. McConnell, "A Review of WTA/WTP Studies," *Journal of Environmental Economics and Management* 44, 3 (November 2002): 426–47.

2. The lawyer Herbert Hovenkamp argues that the difference between WTA and WTP requires the government to supply the poor with the necessities of life. He explains that when it comes to food and shelter, the WTA of the poor, who do not have sufficient quantities of these goods to survive, exceeds the WTP of the rich, who have plenty of these goods. Redistributing these goods will therefore maximize the wealth of society, because the value of these goods is higher when the poor have them. This is a restatement of Bentham's argument with two minor differences. It starts from the assumption that the objective of society is to maximize wealth, and from this objective it derives the conclusion that the only goods that government should redistribute are the necessities of life. But if the objective of society is to maximize society's welfare, then (as Bentham has shown) redistribution should involve all of income and not just the sums necessary for the necessities of life. Herbert J. Hovenkamp, "Legal Policy and the Endowment Effect," *Journal of Legal Studies* 20 (June 1991): 225–47.

3. Pfizer has denied that it had anything to do with the "clearing" of the neighborhood. According to the reporter Ted Mann, its Web site stated, "We at Pfizer have been dismayed to see false and misleading claims appear in the media that suggest Pfizer is somehow involved in this matter . . . the company has no requirements nor interest in the development of the land that is the subject of the case." Mann investigated this claim for the *New London (CT) Day*, and came to doubt it: "Months-long review of state records and correspondence from 1997 and 1998—when officials from the administration of then-Gov. John G. Rowland were helping convince the pharmaceutical giant to build in New London—shows that statement is misleading, at best," he wrote. Ted Mann, "Pfizer's Fingerprints on Fort Trumbull Plan," *New London Day*, October 16, 2005, http://www.freerepublic.com/focus/f -bloggers/1503363/posts (accessed May 26, 2009).

4. "Eminent Domain," National Conference of State Legislators, 2007.

5. A Brief History of the Federal Income Tax

1. "History of the U.S. Tax System," U.S. Department of the Treasury, n.d., http://www.treas.gov/education/fact-sheets/taxes/ustax.shtml (accessed May 26, 2009).

2. Posted at http://www.taxpolicycenter.org/taxfacts/displayafact.cfm?Docid= 213.

6. It Is Not Pareto Efficient

1. Jude Wanniski, "Sketching the Laffer Curve," *Yorktown Patriot* (Denver, CO), June 14, 2005, http://www.yorktownpatriot.com/printer_78.shtml (accessed May 26, 2009).

2. The 70 percent rate (table 4.1) applied to "non-earned" income, such as interest and dividends, not to earned income. But the effect on the work effort, assuming that there is such an effect, should be the same. Why should the rich work hard if their savings are heavily taxed?

3. When the income tax is progressive, each bracket of a person's income is subject to a different tax rate. If income below $500,000 is subject to a 25 percent tax rate and above it to a 50 percent tax rate, then an individual who earns $1 million would owe a tax of $375,000.

4. Martin Feldstein, "Supply Side Economics: Old Truths, New Claims (working paper 1792, National Bureau of Economic Research, Cambridge, MA, January 1986): 4.

5. President Ronald Reagan, "America's New Beginning: A Program for Economic Recovery," White House, February 18, 1981, S-1, http://www .presidency.ucsb.edu/ws/index.php?pid=43427 (accessed June 29, 2009).

6. See summary of the evidence in Austan Goolsbee, "Evidence on the High Income Laffer Curve from Six Decades of Tax Reform," *Brookings Papers on Economic Activity*, issue 2 (1999).

7. Richard Kogan, "The Simple Story: Tax Cuts Lose Revenues," Center for Budget and Policy Priorities, 2004, http://www.cbpp.org/1-25-05bud2.htm (accessed May 26, 2009).

8. Julie Wolf, "The 1982 Recession," *The American Experience*, PBS, n.d. http://www.pbs.org/wgbh/amex/reagan/peopleevents/pande06.html (accessed May 26, 2009).

9. Peter Dreier, "Reagan's Legacy: Homelessness in America," National Housing Institute, May–June 2004, http://www.nhi.org/online/issues/135/ reagan.html (accessed May 26, 2009).

10. Gary K. Clabaugh, "The Educational Legacy of Ronald Reagan," *Educational Horizons*, Summer 2004, http://www.newfoundations.com/Clabaugh/Cut tingEdge/Reagan.html (accessed May 26, 2009).

11. Heather Mac Donald, "Welfare's Next Vietnam," *City Journal*, Winter 1995, http://www.city-journal.org/html/5_1_a1.html (accessed May 26, 2009).

12. Feldstein, "Supply Side Economics," January 1986, p. 3.

13. Bureau of the Census, *American Community Survey*, 2001, 2006; and New York City, "Mayor's Management Report," 2001, 2006.

14. Jennifer Friedlin, "Welfare Series: Block Grants Starve State Budgets," *Women's eNews*, September 3, 2004, http://www.womensenews.org/article .cfm/dyn/aid/1974/context/archive (accessed May 26, 2009).

15. *Paul Lopatto*, "Tuition a Rising Share of CUNY Revenue as State Share Falls," Independent Budget Office, New York City, July 2006, http://www.ibo.nyc .ny.us/iboreports/CUNY_FBjul2006.pdf (accessed May 26, 2009).

16. "Table 319: Average Undergraduate Tuition and Fees and Room and Board Rates Charged for Full-Time Students in Degree-Granting Institutions, by Type and Control," National Center for Educational Statistics, n.d., http:// nces.ed.gov/programs/digest/d06/tables/xls/tabn319.xls (accessed May 26, 2009).

17. U.S. Bureau of the Census, "Historical Income Tables, People, Table P-2: Race and Hispanic Origin of People by Median Income and Sex: 1947 to 2005," *Current Population Survey*, March 2008, http://www.census.gov/hhes/ www/income/histinc/p02.html (accessed May 26, 2009).

18. Cara Mia DiMassa and Richard Winton, "L.A.'s Business Improvement Districts Help Reduce Crime, Study Finds," *Los Angeles Times*, February 20, 2009.

19. Diane Cardwell, "Report Says Ambulances Steer to Their Own Hospitals," *New York Times*, June 27, 2001.

20. Martin Feldstein, "The Effects of Marginal Tax Rates on Taxable Income: A Panel Study of the 1986 Tax Reform," *Journal of Political Economy* 103, 3 (June 1995): 551–71.

21. Louis Lavelle and Ronald Grover, "Exec Perks: An Ugly Picture Emerges," *BusinessWeek*, April 27, 2005.

22. Dean Takahashi, "Hewlett-Packard Leases Two Jets for Its Executives," *San Jose Mercury News*, September 23, 2003, 1.

23. David Cay Johnston, "Assisting the Good Life," *New York Times*, June 15, 2007.

7. Private Goods

1. Joe Wilcox, "Judge Rules Microsoft Violated Antitrust Laws," CNET News April 3, 2000, http://news.com.com/2100-1001-238758.html (accessed May 26, 2009): Wolfgang Gruener, "Firefox sails past 20% market share, IE drops below 70%," *TG Daily* (Monday, December 01, 2008), http://www.tgdaily .com/html_tmp/content-view-40381-113.html.

2. "Earnings: Strong Lipitor Sales Help Quarterly Net Surge 21%," *International Herald Tribune*, July 21, 2005, http://www.iht.com/articles/2005/07/ 20/business/earns.php (accessed May 26, 2009).

3. Jared Bernstein, "Interview with Jared Bernstein," *Multi National Monitor* 24, no. 5 (May 2003), http://multinationalmonitor.org/mm2003/03may/ may03interviewsbernstein.html (accessed May 26, 2009).

4. Marie Connolie and Alan Krueger, "Rockonomics: The Economics of Popular Music," in *Handbook of the Economics of Art and Culture*, ed. Victor Ginsburgh and David Throsby (Boston: Elsevier North-Holland, 2008) 668–716.

5. Alex Williams, "Wedding Singers? Not!" *New York Times*, November 20, 2005.

6. Quoted in Connolie and Krueger, "Rockonomics," 692.

7. James Packard Love, "Notes on Government Role in the Development of HIV/AIDS Drugs," Amicus Curiae, *Pharmaceutical Manufacturers' Association of South Africa and Others v. The President of the Republic of South Africa and Others*, April 10, 2001, http://www.cptech.org/ip/health/sa/loveaffi davit/ (accessed May 26, 2009).

8. Merrill Goozner, "Third World Battles for AIDS Drugs," *Chicago Tribune*, April 28, 1999.

9. John S. James, "South Africa: Glaxo Offers Voluntary License on AZT/3TC," *AIDS Treatment News*, October 19, 2001, http://findarticles.com/p/arti cles/mi_mOHSW/is_2001_Oct_19/ai_79757044 (accessed May 26, 2009).

10. Ceci Connolly "Officials Defend Cost of Medicare Drug Benefit: Importation, Negotiation Ideas Rejected," *Washington Post*, February 17, 2005, A7;

Julie Appleby and Richard Wolf, "Medicare Cost Projections Drop," *USA Today*, February 2, 2006.

11. http://www.singaporeair.com/saa/en_UK/content/exp/A380/Technical
_Specifications.jsp??v=-3644100 4 & (accessed June 29, 2009). "Air Austral Selects A380 in Single-Class Configuration for Future Growth," Airbus press release, January 15, 2009, http://www.airbus.com/en/presscentre/press releases/pressreleases_items/09_01_15_air_austral_a380.html (accessed June 29, 2009).

12. William Neuman, "The Battle of the Biggest," *New York Times*, December 25, 2005.

13. Ibid.

14. Charles Laurence, "Rich and Famous Fall Out of Love with the 'Faulty Towers' of New York," *Daily Telegraph* (London), May 9, 2004.

15. David W. Chen, "A Pool in the Apartment Is the Latest in Extravagance," *New York Times*, April 17, 2004, B1

16. The data for all the charts is from sales. The share of new construction among these observations is therefore higher than the share of new construction in the total inventory of apartments. The U.S. Bureau of the Census conducts a survey of housing in New York City every three years, but it does not collect data about the areas of apartments, which is why data about size must come from sales. How much the increase in apartment size is due to new construction and how much is the result of the assembly of smaller apartments into bigger ones is not known.

17. David Lazarus, "The Doctor Will See You—For a Price," *San Francisco Chronicle*, January 8, 2006.

18. "How We Pay Doctors," *New York Times*, September 6, 2006, A18.

19. Richard Cooper, "Health Affairs," Institute of Health Policy, Medical College of Wisconsin, n.d., cited in Dennis Cauchon, "Medical Miscalculation Creates Doctor Shortage," *USA Today*, March 2, 2005; and Jennifer Cheeseman Day, "Population Projections of the United States, by Age, Sex, Race, and Hispanic Origin: 1993 to 2050," Series P25-1104, U.S. Census, January 18, 2001, http://www.census.gov/prod/1/pop/profile/95/2_ps.pdf.

8. Government-Supplied Goods

1. Zhiqiang Liu, "The External Returns to Education: Evidence from Chinese Cities," *Journal of Urban Economics* 61, no. 3 (May 2007): 542–64.

2. Moshe Adler, "Sometimes, Government Is the Answer," *Los Angeles Times*, March 4, 2006. Further analysis of privatization is available at http://www.columbia.edu/~ma820/privatization.html.

3. Kevin Carey, "The Funding Gap 2004," Education Trust Fund, http://www2.edtrust.org/NR/rdonlyres/30B3C1B3-3DA6-4809-AFB9-2DAACF11CF88/0/funding2004.pdf (accessed May 26, 2009).

4. *Hoke County Board of Education et al. v. State of North Carolina; State Board of Education*, 2000, http://www.schoolfunding.info/states/nc/HOKEI.PDF (accessed May 26, 2009).

5. Rod Paige, "Educational Equality Eludes Us, Even Now," *USA Today*, May 14, 2004, http://www.ed.gov/news/opeds/edit/2004/05142004.html (accessed May 26, 2009).

6. NAEP (National Assessment of Educational Progress), "NAEP 2004 Trends in Academic Progress," 2005, http://nces.ed.gov/nationsreportcard/pdf/main2005/2005463.pdf (accessed May 26, 2009).

7. Richard Rothstein and Karen Hawley Miles, "Where's The Money Gone? Changes in the Level and Composition of Education Spending," Economic Policy Institute, 1995; Richard Rothstein, "Where's the Money Going? Changes in the Level and Composition of Education Spending, 1991–96," Economic Policy Institute, 1997, cited in Kevin Carey, "Education Funding and Low-Income Children: A Review of Current Research," Center for Budget and Policy Priorities, November 5, 2002, http://www.cbpp.org/cms/index.cfm?fa=view&id=1428.

8. Alan Krueger and Diane Whitmore, "Would Smaller Classes Help Close the Black-White Achievement Gap?" (working paper 451, Industrial Relations Section, Princeton University, Princeton, NJ, March 2001), http://www.irs.princeton.edu/pubs/pdfs/451.pdf (accessed May 26, 2009).

9. Ibid.

10. Ibid.

11. *Hoke vs. North Carolina*, 74.

12. Caroline M. Hoxby, "How Much Does School Spending Depend on Family Income?" *American Economic Review* 88, no. 2 (May 1998): 309.

13. Richard Rothstein, "Assessing Money's Role in Making Schools Better," *New York Times*, November 14, 2001.

14. GDP: BEA (Bureau of Economic Analysis), 2008. Population: U.S. Bureau of the Census, 2008.

15. Not all these resources are in the form of cash. Some of the income that people earn and that is part of the GDP is in the form of payments-in-kind. For example, a family that owns its home saves itself the profit that a landlord would have derived from the rent. Poor people are the least likely to have payments-in-kind.

16. Carmen DeNavas-Walt, Bernadette Proctor, Jessica Smith, U.S. Census Bureau, Current Population Reports, P60–235: "Income, Poverty, and Health Insurance Coverage in the United States: 2007," Washington DC, 2008. The poverty threshold is for 2007, whereas the GDP per capita is for 2008. The 2008 threshold will probably be higher than the one for 2007, but the difference will probably be small.

17. Sources: U.S. Bureau of the Census, "American Community Survey, 2007," Table C19101; "Family Income in the Past 12 Months" and Table B19127; "Aggregate Family Income in the Past 12 Months" (calculations by author). The actual proportion of families whose income is less than the average is probably significantly higher than 64 percent because the income variable in the survey does not include payments-in-kind such as those derived from home ownership.

Part II: Introduction

1. In 2007, 146 million Americans worked, and together they produced goods worth $14 trillion. U.S. Bureau of Labor Statistics, CPS 2007, http://data.bls

.gov/cgi-bin/surveymost?1n; and Bureau of Economic Analysis, 2007, http://www.bea.gov/national/xls/gdplev.xls.

2. Lawrence Mishel, Jared Bernstein, and Sylvia Alegretto, *The State of Working America, 2006/7: An Economic Policy Institute Book* [Ithaca, NY: ILR Press, 2007], figure 3F, http://www.stateofworkingamerica.org/tabfig/03/SWA06_Fig3F.jpg (accessed May 26, 2009).

3. Moshe Adler, "Unionization and Poverty. The Case of New York City Retail Workers," Economic Policy Institute, WP 127, December 2003 www.epl.org/workingpapers/wp127.pdf (accessed May 26, 2009).

4. Sarah Anderson, John Cavanagh, Chuck Collins, Sam Pizzigati, and Mike Lapham, "Executive Excess 2008," Institute for Policy Studies and United for a Fair Economy, 2008, http://www.faireconomy.org/files/executive_excess_2008.pdf (accessed May 26, 2009).

9. The Classical Theory of Wages

1. All quotes from Adam Smith, *The Wealth of Nations*, bk. 1, chap. 8, http://www.readprint.com/chapter-8614/Adam-Smith (accessed May 26, 2009).

2. A. Aspinall and E. Anthony Smith, eds., *English Historical Documents*, vol. 11, *1783–1832* (New York: Oxford University Press, 1959), 749–52, http://www.marxists.org/history/england/combination-laws/combination-laws-1800.htm (accessed May 26, 2009).

3. The discussion of Ricardo and of the marginal productivity theory relies heavily on Joan Robinson and John Eatwell, *An Introduction to Modern Economics* (London: McGraw-Hill Book Company, 1973).

4. David Ricardo, "On the Principles of Political Economy and Taxation," chap. 5, *On Wages* (London: John Murray, 1817), http://www.econlib.org/library/Ricardo/ricP2.html (accessed May 26, 2009).

5. See Haim Barkai, "Ricardo on Factor Prices and Income Distribution in a Growing Economy" *Economica*, n.s., 26, no. 103 (August 1959): 240–50.

6. Ibid.

10. The Neo-Classical Theory of Wages

1. "1886, May 4: Haymarket Tragedy," Chicago Public Library http://www.chi publib.org/cplbooksmovies/cplarchive/chidisasters/haymarket.php (accessed May 27, 2009).

2. Following the Haymarket Massacre hangings, May 1 was declared an international labor day and is celebrated in many countries, though not in the United States.

3. John Bates Clark, *The Distribution of Wealth: A Theory of Wages, Interest, and Profits* (New York: Macmillan, 1899), chap. 1, http://www.econlib.org/library/Clark/clkDW1.html (accessed May 26, 2009).

4. Clark, *Distribution of Wealth* chap. 8, http://www.econlib.org/library/Clark/clkDW8.html#VIII.11 (accessed May 26, 2009).

5. "Production Theory Basics," Wikipedia, http://en.wikipedia.org/wiki/Production_theory_basics (accessed May 26, 2009).

6. Angela Chien, "SparkNotes: Labor Demand" http://www.sparknotes.com/economics/micro/labormarkets/labordemand/section1.html (accessed May 26, 2009).

7. Varian, *Intermediate Economics*, 312.

11. The Evidence

1. Gretchen Morgenson, "Pfizer Shareholders Vote to Elect Directors but Show Concern Over Pay," *New York Times*, April 28, 2006. In July 2006 McKinnell was forced to retire early (at age sixty-three, with a $6.5 million/year payment for life). AFL/CIO, "Executive Excess: Final CEO Pay Numbers Reveal Jaw-Dropping Retirement Packages," http://blog.aflcio.org/2006/07/17/executive-excess-final-ceo-pay-numbers-reveal-jaw-dropping-retirement-packages/ (accessed May 26, 2009).

2. Robert Frank, "Are Workers Paid Their Marginal Products?" *American Economic Review* 74 (September 1994): 549–71.

3. Orley Ashenfelter and Štěpán Jurajda, "Cross-Country Comparisons of

Wage Rates: The Big Mac Index," Princeton University and CERGE-EI/ Charles University, October 2001, http://economics.uchicago.edu/down load/bigmac.pdf (accessed May 26, 2009).

12. The Minimum Wage

1. David Card and Alan B. Krueger, "Minimum Wages and Employment: A Case Study of the Fast Food Industry in New Jersey and Pennsylvania," *American Economic Review* 84 (September 1994): 772–93.
2. The authors did not contact McDonald's because it had been unresponsive in a previous survey they had conducted.
3. The reader should be aware that Card and Krueger's results were challenged by economists affiliated with right-wing think tanks, but the challenge has failed. See John Schmitt, "The Minimum Wage and Job Loss: Opponents of Wage Hike Find No Effect," Economic Policy Institute Briefing Paper, 1996.

13. Theories of Wages and the Great Depression

1. John Maynard Keynes, *The General Theory of Employment, Interest, and Money* (London: Royal Economic Society, 1936), chap. 12, http://www .marxists.org/reference/subject/economics/keynes/general-theory/ch12 .htm (accessed May 26, 2009). Recall that we refer to economists who came after Clark's development of the value of marginal product theory of wages as "neo-classical," and to those who preceded him as "classical."
2. Keynes, *General Theory*, chap. 2, http://www.marxists.org/reference/sub ject/economics/keynes/general-theory/ch02.htm (accessed July 29, 2009).
3. Ibid., chap. 12.
4. Gonçalo L. Fonseca, "The Real Balance Debate," The History of Economic Thought Web site, http://cepa.newschool.edu/het/essays/keynes/realbal ances.htm (accessed July 29, 2009).
5. Robert Diamond, "Keynes, IS-LM, and the Marshallian Tradition," *History of Political Economy* 39 (2007): 81–95.

6. Christina Romer, "The Great Crash and the Onset of the Great Depression," *Quarterly Journal of Economics* 105, no. 3 (August 1990): 597–624.

7. U.S. Department of Labor, Bureau of Labor Statistics, Consumer Price Index All Urban Consumers (CPI-U), U.S. city average, ftp://ftp.bls.gov/pub/spe cial.requests/cpi/cpiai.txt (accessed May 26, 2009).

8. Because figures about installed horsepower are not available for the year 1933, the comparison is between the years 1929 and 1935. Bresnahan and Raff suspect, however, that this investment occurred after 1933. Timothy F. Bresnahan and Daniel M. G. Raff, "Intra-industry Heterogeneity and the Great Depression: The American Motor Vehicles Industry, 1929–1935," *Journal of Economic History* 51, no. 2. (June, 1991): 317–31.

14. "Sticky Wages"

1. Axel Leijonhufvud, *On Keynesian Economics and the Economics of Keynes* (London: Oxford University Press, 1968).

2. Milton Friedman, "The Role of Monetary Policy: Presidential Address to the American Economic Association," *American Economic Review* 58 (March, 1968): 1–17; Edmund Phelps, *Microeconomic Foundations of Employment and Inflation Theory* (New York: Norton, 1970).

3. Robert E. Lucas Jr. and Leonard A. Rapping, "Real Wages, Employment, and Inflation," *Journal of Political Economy* 77, no. 5 (September–October 1969): 721–54.

4. Ibid.

5. Albert Rees, "On Equilibrium in Labor Markets," *Journal of Political Economy* 78 (March–April 1970): 308.

6. John Pease and Lee Martin, "Want Ads and Jobs for the Poor: A Glaring Mismatch," *Sociological Forum* 12, no. 4 (1997): 545–64.

7. Press conference, September 18, 1982, American Presidency Project at the University of California, Santa Barbara, http://www.presidency.ucsb.edu/ws/index.php?pid=43062 (accessed May 26, 2009).

8. New York City Department of Parks and Recreation, "Work Experience Program," http://www.nycgovparks.org/sub_opportunities/internships/work_exp_prog_wep.html (accessed May 26, 2009).

9. New York City Law Department, press release, December 4, 2003, http://www.nyc.gov/html/law/downloads/pdf/pr120403.pdf (accessed May 26, 2009).

10. This assumes that the wage the employer offered was not at the minimum to begin with; the wage cannot fall below the costs that a worker incurs when filling it (the cost of having a clean shirt).

11. Arthur Higbee, "American Topics," *New York Times*, September 28, 1992, http://www.iht.com/articles/1992/09/28/topi_7.php. (accessed May 26, 2009). Home Depot's behavior created a Pareto inefficiency. Some owners of very expensive homes may have gone without supplies while owners of shacks may have obtained them instead. But given that in reality without Home Depot's self-imposed price control the poor would have had no supplies and the rich would not have compensated them for their losses, the control was probably efficient in Utilitarian terms; the poor are less able to handle the loss of a house than are the rich.

12. "Delphi's UAW Members Approve Pay-Cut Deal by 68% Vote," Local 2209 Web site, http://www.local2209.org/content/showquestion2006.asp?faq=45&fidAuto=810 (accessed 30 June 2009).

15. "Efficiency Wages"

1. According to Stiglitz, "Though the Great Depression of the thirties was the most recent, prolonged, and massive episode, the American economy suffered major recessions from 1979 to 1982, and many European economies experienced prolonged high unemployment rates during the eighties. Information economics has provided explanations for why unemployment may persist and for why fluctuations are so large. The failure of wages to fall so that unemployed workers can find jobs has been explained by efficiency

wage theories, which argue that the productivity of workers increases with higher wages (both because they work harder and because employers can recruit a higher-quality labor force). If information about their workers' output were costless, employers would not pay such high wages because they could costlessly monitor output and pay accordingly. But because monitoring is costly, employers pay higher wages to give workers an incentive not to shirk." Joseph Stiglitz, "Information," *Concise Encyclopedia of Economics* (2d ed., 2008), http://www.econlib.org/library/Enc/Information.html (accessed May 26, 2009).

2. Dominique Goux and Eric Maurin, "Persistence of Interindustry Wage Differentials: A Reexamination Using Matched Worker-Firm Panel Data," *Journal of Labor Economics*, 17, no. 3 (1999): 492–533.

3. William T. Dickens and Lawrence F. Katz, "Inter-industry Wage Differences and Industry Characteristics," in *Unemployment and the Structure of Labor Markets*, ed. Kevin Lang and Jonathan S. Leonard (New York: Blackwell, 1987), 48–89.

4. If workers get paid a higher wage to give them an incentive not to disrupt the workflow, isn't this a premium for not shirking? If shirking simply means work stoppages while bargaining over the wage, then shirking does take place, and a higher wage is a no-shirking premium. But work stoppages end once the wage has been determined. Workers do not enjoy work stoppages, and it is not the fear of losing their job that prevents them from engaging in them. According to the efficiency wage theory, however, workers always want to shirk, and the only reason they don't is the fear of losing their job.

5. Alan Krueger and Lawrence Summers, "Efficiency Wages and the Wage Structure," The National Bureau of Economic Research, 1986, 26.

6. George Akerlof and Janet Yellen, *Efficiency Wage Models of the Labor Market* (Cambridge: Cambridge University Press, 1990), pp. 2–3.

7. Sam Bowles, "The Production Process in a Competitive Economy: Walrasian, Neo-Hobbesian, and Marxian," *American Economic Review* 1 (March 1985): 33.

8. Daniel M. G. Raff, "Wage Determination Theory and the Five-Dollar Day at Ford," *Journal of Economic History* 48, no. 2 (June 1988): 387–99.

9. Ibid.

16. Executive Compensation

1. Lucian Arye Bebchuk and Jesse M. Fried, "Executive Compensation as an Agency Problem," *Journal of Economic Perspectives* 17, no. 3 (Summer 2003): 71–92.

2. The discussion of GM and Ross Perot is based on Robert A. G. Monks and Nell Minow, *Corporate Governance* (West Sussex: Blackwell, 1995) http://www.ragm.com/books/corp_gov/cases/cs_gm.html (accessed May 26, 2009).

3. Ibid.

4. Ibid.

5. David Ellis and Paul Gray, "Winner of the Week," *Time*, May 14, 1990, http://www.time.com/time/magazine/article/0,9171,970118.00.html (accessed May 26, 2009); Paul Witteman, "Roger's Painful Legacy," *Time*, November 9, 1992 http://www.time.com/time/magazine/article/0,9171,9769 71,00.html (accessed May 26, 2009).

6. Xavier Gabaix and Augustin Landier, "Why Has CEO Pay Increased So Much?" *Quarterly Journal of Economics* 123, no. 1 (2008): 49–100.